...And Jerry Mathers
as "The Beaver"

...And Jerry Mathers as "The Beaver"

Jerry Mathers

WITH HERB FAGEN

BERKLEY BOULEVARD BOOKS, NEW YORK

. . . And Jerry Mathers as "The Beaver"

A Berkley Boulevard Book / published by arrangement with the author

PRINTING HISTORY
Berkley Boulevard trade paperback edition / July 1998

The Penguin Putnam Inc. World Wide Web site address is
http://www.penguinputnam.com

ISBN: 0-425-16370-9

BERKLEY BOULEVARD
Berkley Boulevard Books are published by The Berkley Publishing Group,
a member of Penguin Putnam Inc.,
200 Madison Avenue, New York, New York 10016.
BERKLEY BOULEVARD and its logo are trademarks belonging to
Berkley Publishing Corporation.

PRINTED IN THE UNITED STATES OF AMERICA

10 9 8 7 6 5 4 3 2 1

Contents

Preface

Not long ago I was in the airport waiting to catch a flight. A man walked up to me, politely excused any intrusion, and said, "Aren't you Jerry Mathers?" He said he just wanted to tell me how much he enjoyed *Leave It to Beaver*, and that the show really made an impact on his life. I hear this kind of thing quite often, but this man's story was particularly heartwarming. He told me that his father had recently died, and had been sick for several months before he passed away. So this man took some time off from work to visit his dad. When he arrived, his father was bedridden. So to pass some time they watched *Leave It to Beaver* every day. He mentioned a specific episode where Beaver had to write an essay about his father.

I remembered that show well. It was called "The Most Interesting Character," and is one of my very favorites. In that episode, Beaver's class is assigned a 100-word composition, the subject of which is "The Most Interesting Character I Have Ever Known." Judy Hensler, the class know-it-all and resident tattletale, says she is going to write about her father, whom she claims once shot 50 wild elephants in Africa.

Beaver is puzzled, so Wally suggests that Beaver write about their dad. Ward is just delighted. Yet when Beaver tries and tries to find interesting things to write about Ward, he comes up short. Wally tries to liven up the composition, but nothing seems to work.

When June sees that Beaver is still struggling so hard, she suggests that he try writing about what his father means to *him*, rather than trying to gather a list of interesting things. So Beaver writes the following composition:

The Most Interesting Character I Have Ever Known
BY BEAVER CLEAVER

The most interesting character I have ever known is my father, Mr. Ward Cleaver. He does not have an interesting job, he just works hard and takes care of all of us. He never shot things in Africa, or saved anybody that was drowning, but that's all right with me because when I am sick he brings me ice cream, and when I tell him things or ask him things he always listens to me. He used up a whole Saturday to make things in the garage. He may not be interesting to you or someone else because he's not your father, he's mine.

The guy told me how this really affected him. He suddenly saw that he too had a lot of ideas about his own father. He started thinking about all these special things over the years. These very special things that did not mean anything to anybody else, but were very, very moving to him.

After watching the show together, he said he had a renewed special feeling for his father. Suddenly he remembered all the different things they had done together, those special unsung things his father had done for him, and all those forgotten moments. He became fully aware of his dad for the first time. He told me that had it not been for that particular episode of *Leave It to Beaver*, which they watched together, he might have left unkindled these special little things and precious moments that no one would care about, or even know about. He recalled the time his dad took off work to go to his Little League game, and recognized fully for the first time all the other sacrifices his father had made for him—sacrifices that hitherto had gone unnoticed and underappreciated. I was deeply moved.

Acknowledgments

I would like to express deep appreciation to the following people who helped in the writing of this book by extending their time and granting interviews to the authors. Their comments and anecdotes are interspersed throughout the text, and have added greatly to the story:

Norman Abbott Director, *Leave It to Beaver* and the *New Leave It to Beaver Show*
Frank Bank Clarence "Lumpy" Rutherford
Earl Bellamy Director, *Leave It to Beaver*
Barbara Billingsly June Cleaver
Veronica Cartwright Violet Rutherford
Cher Oscar-winning actress and superstar
Joe Connelly Creator and writer of *Leave It to Beaver*
Richard Correll Richard Rickover
Jennifer Corwin Assistant to Brian McInerney
Patrick Curtis Producer, Curtis Lowe Productions
Nancy Cushing-Jones President, Universal Studios Publishing Division
Tony Dow Wally Cleaver
John Forsythe Actor, *The Trouble with Harry*
Phil Gettleman Tony Dow's manager
Cheryl Holdridge Julie Foster
Ron Howard Actor and award-winning director
Janice Kent Mary Ellen Rogers Cleaver, *Still The Beaver* and the *New Leave It to Beaver Show*
Brian Levant Writer, executive producer, *New Leave It to Beaver Show*
Gretchen Mathers My youngest daughter
Jimmy Mathers Actor, director, and cameraman; my brother
Marilyn Mathers Mother and designated family historian
Mercedes (Merci) Mathers My eldest daughter

Susie Mathers McSweeney Former child model and actress; my
    sister
Brian McInerney My business manager
Eric Osmond Freddie Haskell, *New Leave It to Beaver Show*
Ken Osmond Eddie Haskell
Ted Turner Board of Directors, Time/Warner
Beverly Washburn Actress, "The Blind Date Committee"

—Jerry Mathers
Los Angeles, California, 1998

My deep appreciation to the Museum of Television and Radio
in Beverly Hills, California, for access to its splendid episodic
collection of *Leave It to Beaver* and the *New Leave It to Beaver*, as
well as related documentaries, galas, and tributes. The same appreciation to Cary O'Dell and the staff at The Museum of Broadcast Communication in Chicago for extending their services and
resources.

    My thanks to the archivists at UCLA Film School, and to
Ned Comstock at the University of Southern California for his
enormous help in providing valuable resource data. To my
agent, Jake Elwell of Wieser & Wieser, thanks once more for your
good work and friendship.

    Finally, to Gary Goldstein who first brought me into the
project, to Elizabeth Beier at The Berkley Publishing Group for
her superb editorship and manuscript expertise, and to Barry
Neville who guided the project through its completion, my deep
and sincere appreciation.

—Herb Fagen
Walnut Creek, California,
1998

chapter 1
Looking Back

I remember the Cleavers—June, Ward, Wally and the Beaver—as a fun, typical, all-American family. *Leave It to Beaver* entertained us while reinforcing wholesome family values.

—President Jimmy Carter to Jerry Mathers, March 18, 1997

"What Happened to Family TV?" So read the caption on the cover of the July 13, 1996 issue of *TV Guide*. Many people are asking that same question today, and it's a valid concern to be sure. Yet what I found most revealing in that particular issue of *TV Guide* was the photograph on the cover. Draped across the cover in a resplendent montage of red, white and blue, is Barbara Billingsly, Jerry Mathers and the American Flag in a setting worthy of what is best in the entire *Leave It to Beaver* scrapbook.

Leave It to Beaver has become a cherished cog of our television heritage, and I'm proud to be a lasting part of that wonderful tradition. Parents who watched the show with their children are today's grandparents, even great grandparents. Yesterday's children are today's parents.

It's been forty-one years since the Cleavers hit town, and the American viewing public was introduced to a young boy, his big brother, and their parents. And that family turned out to be what every family in the United States wanted: innocence, optimism, respectability, and adventure. The pleasures were simple and the values were constant.

The show made household names of Barbara Billingsly, Hugh Beaumont, Tony Dow, and Jerry Mathers as the "Beaver." Pundits have suggested that I am the most famous TV kid of the 1950s and 1960s. Certainly I'm honored to have been able to bring Beaver Cleaver to life through 234 half-hour episodes for a period of six years in the late 1950s and early 1960s.

But in reality, the Cleavers were merely four actors with differing backgrounds and varied styles. Two were kids. Two were adults. None of us could ever have imagined that October night in 1957, that our TV family, the Cleavers of Mayfield, USA, would remain ever-popular. And then, through the process of syndication and re-runs, become the second longest running show in TV history, after *I Love Lucy*.

In a broader sense, however, my story is also the saga of a changing America: an America that has survived ten U.S. Presidents, the legacy of Korea and *Sputnik*, of Vietnam and Watergate. It provides a graphic historical time line of evolving institutions and expanding times. It is the story of a society in flux.

When the Cleavers entered your living rooms some forty-one years ago, it was to a vastly different America. By 1957, the so-called baby boomers had reached puberty and had become a distinct cultural force in their own right. And life, they tell us, was so much easier. Ike and Mamie were in the White House, and rock and roll was here to stay. The country was in the twilight of its innocence, and the dark clouds of the 1960s seemed light-years away. As Irwyn Applebaum so aptly suggests in *The World According to Beaver*, if the 1960s was the era of Eldridge Cleaver, then the 1950s was the era of Beaver Cleaver. Automobiles were large and garish in 1957, girls' skirts were stylish and long. Men's hair was usually short, except perhaps for aspiring juvenile delinquents whose long hair met at the back in a DA (duck's ass) haircut.

Elvis Presley was the undisputed king of the teenage set. Five singles including "All Shook Up," "Jailhouse Rock," and "Teddy Bear" headed the year's Top 40 tunes. Not far behind was clean-cut Pat Boone with three singles, "Love Letters in the Sand," "April Love," and "Don't Forbid Me," an indication that romance was still alive and well among the young. Buddy Holly gave us "Peggy Sue," The Diamonds gave us "Little Darling," and Paul Anka sang about "Diana." Harry Belefonte offered a popular taste of Calypso, and the Big Band sound made its last hurrah that year when Jimmy Dorsey's recording of "So Rare" reached number two on the pop charts on June 17, 1957.

In the world of film, *The Bridge on the River Kwai* won eight Academy Award nominations in 1957, including an Oscar for Best Picture of the Year. But the biggest media frenzy was reserved for *Peyton Place*, 20th Century-Fox's Oscar-nominated answer to the sizzling best-selling novel of the same name. Alec Guiness and Joanne Woodward were named the year's Best Actor and Actress. Comedian Red Buttons made a career comeback, winning a Best Supporting Oscar for *Sayonara*, while "All the Way," from *The Joker Is Wild*, was named the movies' Best Song.

In baseball, the Braves dethroned the Yankees as World Champs in 1957, but, unlike today's team, they resided in Milwaukee. Here in Los Angeles, we were anticipating the arrival of Major League Baseball, as the Brooklyn Dodgers were leaving their hallowed home in Ebbets Field to become Southern California's first Major League Baseball team.

"Baseball, motherhood and apple pie" was still a prevailing ethos in 1957, if I'm allowed a bit of literary license. There were drive-in movies and corner soda shops, white bucks and "purple people eaters." There were movie shows and skating rinks, LP records and transistor radios. But increasingly, people were turning to TV as their prime diversion. Forty million TV sets could be found in family homes across the country in 1957—quite a leap from the ten thousand or so TV sets just a decade earlier.

When *Leave It to Beaver* made its debut on October 4, 1957, CBS mounted no major promotional campaign. While the reviews were generally good, they were not outstanding. There was little indication that a permanent slice of our popular culture was being defined. Nor did we have any idea that our personal and professional lives would change forever.

John Crosby in the *New York Herald Tribune* was enthusiastic, calling the show "charming and sincere," with a "wonderful candor and directness with which children disconcert and enchant you." *TV Guide* enjoyed it too, proclaiming *Leave It to Beaver* the "sleeper of the 1957–58 season." On the other hand, the *New York Times* was only lukewarm, and questioned the show's appeal as "being too broad and artificial to be persuasive."

We even managed to get into a bit of trouble with the CBS censors, if you can believe that. The result was that the first episode had to be shelved for one week because we allowed a toilet to be seen on the small screen. We were to debut with an episode called "Captain Jack." The boys, Wally and the Beav, send for an alligator. They don't want Ward and June to know they have an alligator, so they hide it in the toilet tank. When it was time to release the series, the episode was banned by the CBS censors, who found it lacking good taste because some scenes actually showed the interior of a bathroom.

The CBS censors said, "Absolutely not!" They could not do the show, they insisted, because there was a TV code forbidding shots of a bathroom on TV. We had a big problem, though, because there was no other place the kids could hide an alligator. Well, the censors went round and round on the issue, before reaching a compromise. They agreed we could show the toilet tank, but nothing else. So *Leave It to Beaver* became the first television show where the house actually had a bathroom. *The Brady Bunch* of the 1970s didn't even have a toilet.

I'm often asked to comment on the enduring appeal of *Leave It to Beaver*. What sets our show apart from the other fine situation comedies of its era? Why has the show touched a positive chord in so many people, for such a long time? I'm not sure I can supply all the answers, but I will at least give it a try.

Let's start by saying that our generation of TV kids were the first child actors to grow up in your living rooms. Sure, the movies presented lots of great child stars over the years: Jackie Coogan, Freddie Bartholomew, Deanna Durbin, Mickey Rooney, Judy Garland, Margaret O'Brien, Butch Jenkins, Shirley Temple, Jane Withers, and Jackie Cooper. But for most families, movies were a big event. You had to dress up, go out, and pay money to see a show. The movie houses could be elaborate and grand,

and your stars bigger than life. They towered over you, thirty-five feet tall at times. Television changed all that. Kid actors like Tony Dow, Ken Osmond, and me, in fact all the TV kids of the 1950s, appeared on a small screen right in front of you in your living rooms. We grew up before your eyes just like people you really knew.

But what made our show so unique were the writers and creators of *Leave It to Beaver*, Joe Connelly and Bob Mosher. Mr. Connelly and Mr. Mosher came from radio where they were the best in the business. They were able to bring a totally different and fresh perspective to *Leave It to Beaver*. Writing for radio, Connelly and Mosher wrote a fifteen minute show every day. They had to be aware of the theater of the mind on radio. The jokes had to work because of what people heard, not what they saw. They were masters of dialogue—good, crisp, clever dialogue. *Leave It to Beaver* provided them with the luxury of an entire week to shoot one episode. They could go back and fine tune a whole lot more than they could in radio. We had a wonderful cast and some of the most outstanding directors in the business, but it was the creative genius of Joe Connelly and Bob Mosher, more than any other factor, that set *Leave It to Beaver* apart from all the other family sitcoms.

Leave It to Beaver also brought a new perspective to the situation comedy. It presented a child's view of the world. Other popular shows like *Father Knows Best, Make Room for Daddy*, and *The Donna Reed Show* depict adults looking at children. *Leave It to Beaver*, on the other hand, presents the inequities and confusion of the adult world being forced upon a child.

The Beaver is an everyman kind of innocent character who walks through life, never really doing anything that he deems bad. But he is very gullible and innocent, and consequently a lot of his friends talk him into doing things he might not do on his own. His family is his haven of safety, his home his pantheon of security. Here he finds the conventional wisdom of his father Ward, the gentle understanding of his mother June, and the soothing yet confusing camaraderie of Wally. Here he finds love.

Today's sitcom is very different. Today, most shows are joke-driven. *Leave It to Beaver* was driven by plot and dialogue. Just

watch a few re-runs today. There are very few one-liners put in
there just for laughs.

Leave It to Beaver was not a one-dimensional show either.
There were several plots, not just one main theme. Wally is doing
one thing; the Beaver is doing something else; Ward and June
are interacting with each other or with the boys. Many things
are going on. The stories move along smoothly, and the cadence
is evenly paced. Each show had a moral—a lesson. Not the big
kind that hits you over the head. Instead they were like medieval
morality plays. You sit there and watch. The characters do things
and there are consequences for their actions. There is a cause
and effect. The situations and themes varied, but the moral always seemed to be, "Do the right thing!" Just that simple.

We also tackled some very interesting themes that are tepid
by today's standards, but really were ahead of their time. For
example, we had a show on alcoholism. We had a show on people from different cultures. A favorite show of mine dealt with
divorce.

In this episode Beaver has a friend named Chopper whose
parents are divorced. He tells Beaver that it is wonderful. At
Christmastime he gets presents from all his stepdads and step-
moms; he seems so happy because he gets all these great presents. So Beaver asks Ward, "Why don't you get divorced so that
I can get all these presents?" Ward takes Beaver into the den and
says, "Do you want to break up our happy family just to get
presents? Because we'd all be separated if we did." Very simple
yet very poignant.

Such topics were rarely touched on in other sitcoms of our
era. Of course, they are done very blatantly today, but not nearly
as well, I feel. Our presentations were subtle and far more effective.

I think that the enormous popularity of the show continues
for the most basic reason: people can truly relate to it. They can
relate to it because Beaver did things that really happen to kids.
Give or take a certain amount of gloss and embroidery, things
that happened to a kid in the 1950s, could have happened to
kids in the 1930s, 1960s, 1970s or 1980s as well.

The problems facing Beaver and Wally were real and universal. Tony Dow never left the industry and is a fine director today. We often talk about the remarkable qualities and subtext of the shows. Our messages were subtle, but they left a mark. Tony and I have been good friends since I met him in 1957. There are people out there today who still think Tony and I really are brothers. I think it may be because of Rick and David Nelson of *Ozzie and Harriet*. They find it hard to believe that Tony isn't my real brother and that the Cleavers were not a real family. They believe that the people in Mayfield really existed, and things that happened on the show really did happen. Kids and adults often tell me that one particular show is their favorite. What is funny is that it is usually never the same show. I ask them why that particular show is their personal favorite. The reason they frequently give is: "When I was a kid, the same thing happened to me."

The most interesting part of the entire Beaver phenomenon to me is its durability. People as diverse as George Foreman and Ringo Starr have remained Beaver fans and are happy to say so publicly.

I've been told that *Leave It to Beaver* has been seen in eighty countries, and has been translated into forty different languages. That's probably an accurate assessment. In Montreal last year, where most of the people speak French, I was asked to appear on radio. I told them that I really couldn't speak a word of intelligible French. They were neither dissuaded nor disconcerted. They simply called for an interpreter to translate my every word.

Another time I was flying back home from an engagement. The guy sitting next to me kept looking at me. Finally he said, "I know you. You're Jerry Mathers." He explained that he was a bush pilot and flew copies of *Leave It to Beaver* all over Africa. He said that in Africa the show aired in several countries, and was heard in seven or eight different languages.

The show is very popular in Japan too. In Japan they use a little girl's voice for the Beav, which is fine for the first few years but by the last year I'm thirteen and still speaking Japanese with a little girl's voice. Every two or three years I get a flood of letters from Japan, and they are exactly the same. This is because the Japanese teen magazines publish the letters in English, and fans copy them word for word. The Japanese are so meticulous that they always copy it the exact same way. I might get a letter that reads: "Dear Mr. Mathers: I love the show *Leave It to Beaver*." The only thing that's different in each letter is the name and address at the end. Yet it's always in perfect English. I must get 150 to 250 letters from Japan on a regular basis requesting an autographed picture.

Strangely enough, England is the one English-speaking country that has never run the *Leave It to Beaver* show. I'm not sure why, but over the years I've heard stories that suggest that the BBC thought it was an unrealistic portrait of American youth. I've gone to England several times for pleasure and business. No one recognizes me. I can go around completely anonymous. It's one of the very few places I can walk around all day and do all sorts of things, and no one pulls me over. Waiters sometimes come up to me in a restaurant and ask, "Should I know you?" I'll reply, "No, I don't think so." Then they tell me that while I don't look familiar to them, the tourists at the next table would like to have my autograph. It seems that tourists are about the only people in England who ever ask me for an autograph.

I do a lot of speaking at colleges these days. At the end of my talk I go out and sign autographs. Many kids from Southeast Asia come up and say that they learned English by watching *Leave It to Beaver*. Because of all the different dialects spoken in Asia the show is televised in English and subtitled. So while these college students are learning English, the dialect they are learning is 1950s Valley Talk.

Given all this appeal, a surprising fact is that *Leave It to Beaver* never made TV's top-ten during its original run. At first, it was aired a little later at night and a lot of kids missed it. But when it went into reruns it was able to reach everyone. Three years ago, if you lived in Los Angeles and had cable TV, you could watch *Leave It to Beaver* five hours a day. When it was on prime time, it was on only a half hour a week and the viewing audience was far more limited.

It befuddles my imagination. Everyone in America, from Presidents to corporate moguls to rock stars to blue collar workers like to talk about what my career meant to their lives. In recent years I have made many appearances on the *Tonight Show*. On one occasion I made George Foreman an honorary citizen of Mayfield. Another time Jay Leno had me playing Beavis and had a cartoon Butthead next to me. We have done all kinds of crazy sketches on the *Tonight Show*. Jay and I have lots of good-natured fun together.

In many ways I was a kid born at the right time and in the right place. The struggles were there from the start. People say what a natural I was, yet I battled the pangs of dyslexia. Battling to compensate, I studied hard and earned a degree in Philosophy from the University of California at Berkeley. Then I went on to a successful business career in banking and real estate before re-entering show business later in life.

I have worn many hats, other than the cherished green base-ball cap (did you know it was green? Hard to tell on a black and white show, I guess.) from *Leave It to Beaver*. My travels and experiences have taken me far beyond the mythical boundaries of Mayfield, USA, and the Cleaver household, be it 485 Maple Drive or 211 Pine Street.

I'm an independent thinker who prides himself in not fol-lowing the flock. I'm a member of the NRA, I love to hunt, and I am a firm believer in the Second Amendment. I served my country proudly as a member of the Air National Guard during the Vietnam War. To play on the words of Mark Twain, reports of my combat death in Vietnam were greatly exaggerated.

I left show business in 1963 to attend Notre Dame High School, where my dad had been a coach and a teacher. I just wanted to be a regular kid. I've been very lucky. Unlike many of my generation of kid actors, I was blessed with a stable family life. My brother Jimmy, who was born in 1955, followed me into show business. In the 1960s he was the star of the television series *Ichabod and Me*, and has continued in the industry as an actor, producer, director, and now a skilled cameraman. My sis-ter Susie became a child model like me and did lots of TV work. In 1954 we worked together in the movie *This Is My Love* with Linda Darnell and Dan Dureya. A mother of three, Susie teaches kindergarten in Westlake Village, California, today. My two youngest brothers, Shaun and Patrick, followed my brother-in-law Bill McSweeney into law enforcement. We have family get-togethers on a regular basis. On August 9, 1997, my mom and dad, Norman and Marilyn Mathers, celebrated their Golden Wedding Anniversary. What a wonderful blessing for all of us.

Still, life has accorded me my proper share of sorrows, doubts, and disappointments. In my late teens I certainly was not St. Jerry Mathers. My parents and I didn't always see eye to eye. As in all families, we had our share of friction. Like all of us approaching our fiftieth year, it's amazing how much smarter my parents seem today than they were back when I was twenty-five.

I have little tolerance and feel somewhat sorry for former child actors who blame their parents for their life's failures. Some of these actors are very bitter people who went on to have problems with drugs and alcohol, even problems with the law. They have asked me to join them on TV shows to talk about their problems, but I have always refused. Maybe their parents were not as supportive as mine. Maybe they didn't try to find other professional opportunities. I simply cannot join their ranks.

People seem to expect, even demand, a certain public persona from me. Perhaps they need to remember Beaver Cleaver as he was. They need the youthful innocence and a bygone era to remain just as it was at the time.

My two marriages ended up in divorce. Let's face it. Being married to a guy who could not go out to dinner or a movie without being approached by fans, some really nice and some rather obnoxious, is no easy task. Every time I was asked to take a picture with someone, they would also ask my wife to get out of the way. Sometimes a person would just push her out of the way. Any celebrity will tell you how angry the nonfamous spouse can get. The only remedy is not to go out all all. The tragic death of Lady Diana Spencer in 1997 was the ultimate example of how the unbalanced life of a celebrity can destroy both a marriage and a life.

Since coming out of self-imposed exile last year, I date occasionally, but it's not easy. If the girl does not recognize me,

The house was recommended to them by Hugh Beaumont, who had become a good friend of the family.

The community around Canoga Park was special. Much of it was still rural. David Butler, one of the show's outstanding directors who earlier in his career had directed Shirley Temple, gave me a quarter horse as a present when we lived in Canoga Park. We had a little stream in the back of the house where my best friend Richard Correll and I played for hours on end, catching toads and tadpoles, playing war, and doing the things kids liked to do. We were a living homage to the modern-day Tom Sawyer/Huckleberry Finn characters that the Beaver and friends have been compared to. Rich Correll played Richard Rickover on *Leave It to Beaver*. Today, Rich is a very successful TV director and we still are close friends.

The day *Leave It to Beaver* aired on TV, *Sputnik* was launched by the Russians. Ours can rightly be viewed as being the first TV show of the Space Age. An astronomer friend tells me that the waves from the original *Leave It to Beaver* now are passing through the Constellation Gemini, in the center of Castor and Pollux, which is thirty-five to forty-five light-years away. If Einstein's theory is basically true, that the universe is expanding, then those waves will go on forever. But if the universe is curved, then those waves will come back to earth. Think what that could mean.

chapter 2

Meet the Mathers

I remember going to visit the Mathers on weekends, and that I didn't want to leave. When I had to go home on Sundays, I'd be depressed about it.

—*Richard Correll*

In the mid 1940s, there was a hit song called "Sioux City Sue," sung by Bing Crosby. A nice song, it appeared on *The Hit Parade* for fourteen weeks in 1946. For most people back then, "Sioux City Sue" was all they really knew about the town of Sioux City, Iowa. My dad Norman Mathers was born there on December 10, 1921.

My dad was one of those all-around guys. He was both a top student and a top athlete. Endowed with strong leadership and athletic abilities, his high school buddies named him "Cappy" because he was usually the team captain, as well as being his high school and college student body president. Born and raised with Midwestern values, my dad's father was a letter carrier (he always refers to him as a letter carrier, not a mailman). My grandmother, a school teacher before she married, gave piano lessons most of her adult life.

My father's Irish/German background, and his upbringing, made him a firm believer in hard work and proper discipline. While in high school, he worked in the Sioux City Stock Yards pitching big bales of hay. This was the ideal job for athletes—a 1930s answer to the weight training programs of today.

I was very lucky. My dad was in some ways a perfect parent for a child who was out of the mainstream. He was the principal of Granada Hills High School, which was the largest high school in the L.A. Unified School District at that time with five thousand students. My dad came through the ranks in the field of education. He received a Master's Degree at the University of Southern California, with a focus on administration. He worked as a teacher, vice principal, and principal, before his promotion as Deputy Superintendent assigned to inner-city L.A. He held this position until he retired. Because of this he was always very up on what kids should and should not be doing. He was trained to deal with boys, working both with the very best of kids and the very worst. Dad knew when something was normal adolescent behavior that he could tolerate and when things were just plain wrong.

My dad was a real hero to us, a figure we equated with John Wayne. He was an Army Air Corps pilot during World War II, and flew missions over Germany. During one off-repeated incident, his plane was damaged by enemy fire and unable to make it back to the field. Fortunately, he found himself and his crew behind their own lines, rather than behind the enemy's.

My father has always been very sensitive to any form of anti-Semitism. Once a Catholic friend told me his father said only Catholics would go to heaven and Jews could not. This worried me because I had Jewish friends. When I told my father what I had been told he got angry. He said that God had a special place for Jewish people. They had died for God. This is a direct result of the war. Toward the war's end, my father was assigned as a pilot to bring back Holocaust victims. He would bring them back to hospitals in Paris. He told me how they kissed him and told him about missing family members. Little girls told him what German guards had done to them. These were French Jews who managed to survive through various Nazi death camps. At night in his dreams he can still see their faces. I can only assume how traumatic and horrifying it was for my father. When he begins to tell the story, he inevitably stops and tears stream down his face. My tough football coach, school-principal dad can never finish telling me about that horrible time in his life.

In our household, Dad ruled the roost. We always had dinner at six o'clock sharp. Families really had dinner together back then; not separately or in front of the TV like today. If you weren't home for dinner, you'd better have a good excuse. My dad would sit at the head of the table where he could see the door. If you walked in at five minutes past six, watch out! The smallest kid, or the kid most prone to cause trouble, would have to sit right next to my dad. As you got older, and hopefully more well behaved, you got to move further away from him.

While my dad stayed true to his Midwestern roots, my mother became a southern Californian at a much earlier age. She was born Marilyn Donna Bright in the small town of Keewatin, near Hibling, in Northern Minnesota in 1927. Her father Kenneth, a chemist, died when she was four years old. One particular Minnesota winter was so severe that her mother, Marie (first generation Irish), decided to move to California where she had relatives living in Los Angeles. My grandmother owned a little Model A Ford that my grandfather bought her just before he died. She packed all their belongings, got someone to put a rack on the top of the car, and placed her two little girls in the backseat. She drove by herself over the rugged Rockies, before finally reaching Los Angeles.

Someone in Minnesota had told my mother and my aunt Colleen that the streets were paved with gold in California. My grandmother drove straight through the last night on the road, and when my mom and my aunt woke up the next morning in California, they were disappointed not to find gold on the streets. They had to settle for some orange groves instead.

My grandmother always had a dream of being a dress designer. So she enrolled in the Lipman School of Design. The tuition and the family's living expenses took a big bite out of her husband's insurance. After living in Los Angeles for a year, my grandmother moved to a nice neighborhood in Hollywood where she found a comfortable one bedroom flat on Wilton Avenue. She had hoped that she could get a job at a studio in the wardrobe department. But it was 1935, the height of the Depression, and jobs were few and far between. Within a year, their money dwindled and they were forced to go on public assistance.

My grandmother was a very proud woman, and like most of the people of her generation was ashamed to be on welfare. The financial hardship was kept a secret, and my grandmother never revealed it to anyone. She dressed herself and her two daughters well, and kept up a good front at all times. Back then people could be poor and still live with dignity. Hollywood was basically a laid back city where people could walk any place at any time, with little fear, and in relative comfort. There was no homeless problem and very little crime.

My mother went to Hollywood High School. While a lot of her classmates had parents in the film industry, she was never particularly interested in it. But my aunt Colleen got a job in the publicity department at Paramount Studios, so in time my mother had a pretty good understanding of the movie business.

After classes or on Saturdays she and her girlfriends would go to CBS and NBC and get tickets for the big radio shows. She saw Glenn Miller, Mickey Rooney, and a very young Frank Sinatra, then the reigning teenage heartthrob. In the early and mid 1940s, teenage girls would scream for Frank Sinatra, with the same verve and passion as they did for Elvis Presley in the 1950s, and the Beatles in the 1960s.

Mom had two friends at Hollywood High who were sisters and lived a few blocks away. They would brag incessantly about their handsome cousin in Sioux City, Iowa, who was not only good looking, but smart and athletic as well. He liked Southern California so much, he would make it a point to visit them every year. His name was Norm Mathers.

It was wartime, and patriotism was running high. The Big Band sounds of Glenn Miller, The Dorseys, and Harry James flooded the airwaves; so did the soothing voices of Bing Crosby, Dick Haymes, Frank Sinatra, and Kate Smith.

In Morningside, a suburb of Sioux City, twenty-year-old Norman Mathers had two years of college behind him. He enlisted in the Army, and was sent to Santa Ana, California, for his Air Corps Cadet training. In those years, the Air Force was a branch of the United States Army, and called the Army Air Corps.

One evening there was a knock on my mother's door. It was her two friends' older brother. There was another fellow too: a tall good looking guy in a military uniform. Mom was still in high school, and was ready for bed. Embarrassed beyond belief because her hair was in pin curlers, she quickly told them that her sister (my aunt Colleen) wasn't home, and shut the door. Anyhow, she didn't like officers, she told her friends, because "they were too old and thought they were hot stuff." The guy in uniform of course was cousin Norm Mathers, and Mom would not see him again until after the war.

So Norman Mathers went off to war and flew missions over Germany. A decorated soldier, he returned to Morningside College in Iowa after the war to continue his education. Marilyn Bright had graduated from Hollywood High in 1945, and received a scholarship to Immaculate Heart College, a Catholic women's college located where the American Film Institute is today.

One of Norm's West Coast cousins decided to get married, and Norman came to the wedding. My mom and dad were introduced again. They started dating, then started dating seriously. They became engaged, and on August 9, 1947, they were married in the Catholic Church. Both were practicing Roman Catholics, and remain so today. In fact, my mother is a past president of the Los Angeles Council of Catholic Women, and until very recently—and as far back as I can remember—my dad ushered at 8:00 Mass every Sunday morning.

At the time they were married, my father had already signed his first teaching contract at Rock Rapids High School in Iowa. So my parents returned to Sioux City, and that's where I enter the story. I was born on June 2, 1948. Four more children, one sister and three brothers, would follow.

But the lure of Southern California never abated. When my aunt wrote to my folks to tell them that Notre Dame High School was being built in the Valley, my dad eagerly applied there for a job. He had all the right credentials, and the brothers were impressed. The job was his. When Notre Dame High School opened its doors in September 1949, my dad was on the faculty as a teacher and a coach. We rented a little white bungalow in Hollywood, not far from Paramount Studios.

William L. O'Neill, the distinguished historian and author, has called the years between 1945 and 1960 "The American High." He's right on target, I think. People like my mother and father, those who experienced the hardships of the Great Depression and the noble sacrifice of World War II, were now raising families of their own. The boys had come home, and the GI Bill allowed men like Norm Mathers to return to school and carve out careers. People were very idealistic after World War II. It was a period of cautious optimism. Men came back from service to a changing America. They were determined to start families of their own, and to provide a better future for their own children than their parents had been able to provide for them.

The postwar generation was listening to such songs as "A Tree in the Meadow," "It's Magic," and "Buttons and Bows," the Oscar-winning song from the movie *Paleface*, starring Jane Russell and Bob Hope. Other popular films in 1948 included *The Treasure of the Sierra Madre* (one of my top-ten favorites), *One Touch of Venus*, and *Johnny Belinda*, which garnered Best Actress honors for Jane Wyman. By the time production was over, Jane Wyman and husband Ronald Reagan were divorcing. "I think I'll name Johnny Belinda co-respondent," the future President quipped to reporters.

Those of us who were born in the immediate postwar period would one day come to be labelled "Baby Boomers," and for better or for worse we too would leave our own distinct mark.

My mother and dad did a good job of preserving many of the Mathers family's amusing anecdotes and heartfelt stories. My mom is the designated and official family historian.

Since she never wanted a show business career for herself, my mother didn't have such dreams for her children. Unlike many mothers who held these aspirations for their own kids, or were compensating for their own failed aspirations, my mom's only burning desire was to be a good mother and loving parent. I believe one of the main reasons I was a successful child actor was because my parents knew the importance of discipline. Their discipline was mainly a loving discipline, not the physical type. Never having been spanked as a child herself, my mother looked askance at spanking her own kids.

One of the ironies of *Leave It to Beaver* is that while I was the youngest brother in the Cleaver household, I was the oldest brother in the Mathers household. Conversely, Tony Dow who played my older brother on the show, was actually the youngest in his family.

It seems like the only thing I did on time as an infant was to learn to walk. I walked at about nine months, but I was also a very cautious kid and wouldn't let go of my mom's hand. I did not really walk alone until I was eleven months. My mother also worried because I didn't talk much. My dad's cousin had a child just weeks older than I was. At a family birthday party, with lots of kids around the same age, about all I could say was "Mommy and Daddy." The other kids could say things like, "bow-wow," "kitty," and "doggie." It wasn't my best performance. To compound matters I didn't get teeth until about nine months, roughly three months later than other kids. Because I was a first child, my mother worried about all these things. Only after I married and had children of my own did I fully appreciate all her concerns.

One day, when I was about fifteen months old, my mother was feeding me, and she got a bit of a shock when I said to her, "I want more peas." It was the first sentence I ever spoke. From then on I somehow started saying everything in sentences. When my mom took me to a two year birthday party for the same little cousin, she said to herself, "My gosh! These other little kids are really going to be talking now." But when we got there, she found that these same kids couldn't say any more than they did when they were a year old, and here I was talking in sentences.

I was also precocious. When I was just a toddler, my parents rented a house in Hollywood. I was walking around outside and saw what I thought was a bomb attached to the house. Because I was sure it was a time bomb, I went inside and got a hammer. Then I went back outside and started pounding and pounding the bomb so it wouldn't explode. Well, the bomb turned out to be the gas meter, and I nearly destroyed it.

I was blessed with a good memory and a long attention span. My father's aunt had a TV set, and at just a year old I would sit through whole episodes of *Kukla, Fran and Ollie,* one of the most popular TV shows of the early 1950s. The next year, they started showing Hopalong Cassidy and cowboy movies on television. Hoppy was my hero and I would happily sit through a whole movie. Later, Roy Rogers became my Number One cowboy hero. My parents would read to me every night before I went to bed. My favorite story was *Five Little Firemen,* which was one of the Golden Books series. It was a cute tale about a little fat lady that couldn't get out the window. My mother sometimes accidentally skipped a page, and I always knew that she had skipped it.

When I was two and a half, we went to my aunt's house for Christmas. There was a little girl who had come there from Iowa. She was older than I was, perhaps six or seven years old. Her father was so proud that she could sing a song. I believe she sang "White Christmas." Everyone was making a big fuss about her, and her father gave her 50 cents. Her father said, "Jerry, do you know anything?" It seems that my mom had read "The Night Before Christmas" to me a few times. She thought I knew about four or five lines. So when I got up and recited the entire "Night Before Christmas," everyone was simply amazed. Her father gave me 50 cents. It was the first money I ever received for performing.

As a boy, I loved dogs. (In fact, my sister Susie actually became "Susie" because of a dog.) In the mid 1950s, *Rin Tin Tin* was a very popular show. I was a big fan of Lee Aaker who played Rusty, and I wanted more than anything else to have a dog like Rin Tin Tin. Little did any of us know at the time that my childhood passion for a dog would save all our lives.

The Dog Story—as I call it—has to do with my family, my parents, and the work ethic they taught me. It was a family policy that whenever I worked they would reward me. Even when I was a model, my parents would buy me something each time I worked.

When we moved to Canoga Park, my parents agreed that
we could get a dog. But my dad said that we couldn't afford a
dog like Rin Tin Tin because he was a thoroughbred. I said I
only wanted a dog like Rin Tin Tin. My dad made me a deal. If
I got another job and made enough money, then he would buy
me a dog like the one I wanted. Lo and behold, that night John
Engstead, a top photographer, called and said he had a modeling
job for me. So suddenly my dad was stuck. He had promised
me that if I got a job, I could get a dog like Rin Tin Tin.

He looked in the classified ads to see if there was a German
Shepherd with the same bloodline as Rin Tin Tin for sale. He
found one, and we were all so excited, but the big problem was
just how much money it would cost. Our deal was that we
would spend only the amount that I would make on the modeling job. When we arrived at the breeder's place, he showed us
a litter of about seven puppies, who were playing with each
other on the grass. As I approached, one puppy's ears went up
and he came running over to me, jumped up on me and wanted
to play. At that moment he captured my heart and that was the
dog I knew was meant to be mine. I told them my choice and
they said, "Oh, you better choose another dog. That one's the
pick of the litter and he would cost more than the other puppies." I went home heavy-hearted fearing the dog of my dreams
was too expensive. Then we received the check in the mail for
the modeling job and it was twice the rate I usually got. Turns
out it was for an especially important client and John Engstead,
generous man that he was, shared the windfall with the models.
So we paid for the dog, and took him home. I named the dog
Ron-Ton-Ton.

About three years later we were all asleep in the house. The
hallway connected all the bedrooms, and the only way to exit
was through the hallway. The dog slept by the front door. That
night when we were all asleep, a part in the forced-air heater
blew up and flames began to shoot up the roof and creep
through the hallway. Eventually the entire hallway became en-
gulfed in flames. Because the heater didn't blow up with a lot
of noise, we didn't wake up. Ron-Ton-Ton, sensing the danger,
ran through the hallway, right through all the flames, and began

licking my father's face until he woke up. The fire department said if we hadn't gotten out of the house when we did, we all would have died. So the reason the family is alive today is because of my finding this wonderful German shepherd.

On February 9, 1951, my sister Susie was born. Although everybody has always called her Susie, her real name isn't Susie at all. It's Marilyn. Here we have another dog story. One of our neighbors had a dog named Susie. I liked it and would always call out to it. My little sister picked up on this. She was about a year and a half now and people would come up to her and say things like, "What a cute little girl! What's your name?" And she'd say, "My name is Susie!" And she's been Susie ever since.

And the family kept on growing: my brother Jimmy was born May 5, 1955; my brother Shaun on March 7, 1963 (before the last episode of *Leave It to Beaver*); and my brother Patrick was born on December 23, 1964.

chapter 3

A Trouper at Two

As we know in our business, young actors' mothers can be pains in the ass, and they generally are. They live vicariously through the child. They bring about—in more cases than not—terrible confusion, anxiety, and neurosis in the child. Jerry's mother treated him in the ideal way a young actor should be treated.

—*John Forsythe*

John Dos Passos once wrote that a person does not choose a career, a career chooses the person. In my case, this is very true because my acting career was just an accident. In more cases than not, I happened to be in the right place at the right time.

Because I am so identified with *Leave It to Beaver*, I will forever remain "the Beav" to most people, both in and out of the industry. But I was already a show business veteran by the time the series debuted in 1957, having made my first television appearance in 1951 at the ripe old age of two and a half.

Susie was on the way, and my mother decided to go downtown to shop for a maternity dress. Because my dad had the only car in the family then, we did most of our traveling by bus when he wasn't home. My mother was always concerned about how her children looked, just as my grandmother had been. Because we were taking the bus and would be out in public, she made sure I looked as spiffy as possible. She dressed me in a coordinated pair of pants and a shirt, and polished up my white-top shoes. We boarded the bus headed toward the Broadway Department Store in downtown Los Angeles.

We were walking through the Broadway with my mother holding my hand, when a lady stopped us. "Why don't you take your little boy up to the tenth floor," she said. "The store is looking for children for their Christmas catalogue." According to the lady, the store wanted to put together a poster-book family for its catalogue cover, and I resembled some of the older children. She instructed my mother to see a Mrs. Bell on the tenth floor. My mom pondered for a few seconds, then decided to take the chance. When we entered Mrs. Bell's office, we came face-to-face with a severe looking lady who resembled an old-fashioned fire and brimstone schoolmarm. She started barking orders. I was to walk over here, then I was to walk over there. I was to turn around, then I was to walk back. She asked my mother what size shoe I wore, what size suit, and what size shirt. All the time she was writing things down and talking notes.

My mother had the distinct impression that they were going to use me. But when we got home we heard nothing for almost a week. Finally, on a Friday at 9 P.M., we received a call from Mrs. Bell. She told my mom to bring me to a designated place on Wilshire Boulevard. It was to be my first foray into the world of show business.

When we arrived, we found all kinds of kids and their parents. There was a baby who was crying all the time, a little girl who was about my age, and quite a few older boys who were ages seven to ten. My mother brought our little Golden Books with us so she could read to me while we waited. First they took the baby, the one who was crying all the time. Then the little girl started running, so they took her next. Then there were the older boys. Their mothers were typical Hollywood mothers. They bellowed incessantly that they had other interviews, and their kids were being delayed.

By now everybody was out of there. They looked at me and called me front and center. Well, I had been watching all the older boys marching up to the front, finding their mark, then putting their hands in their pockets. So I did just the same. The photographer was amazed. He couldn't believe it. I had been so impressed with the bigger kids that I wanted to be just like them. "This kid's terrific," the photographer said. "Who's his agent?"

Of course I didn't have an agent. The photographer was named Lyman Emerson, one of the top photographers in town. He told my mother that he had an old friend with an agency for children, called the Screen Children's Guild. So at the age of two my professional career began with my first photos appearing in the 1951 Christmas Catalogue for the Broadway Department Store.

Lyman Emerson used me in ads for a lot of his top clients, such as S.O.S pads and Sunkist oranges. He pitched me for Desmonds, one of the best-known department stores in Los Angeles. I became a Desmonds regular, appearing week after week in the newspaper ads and holiday catalogues. Meanwhile, my mother was flooded with calls from other photographers who wanted me for other magazines. I became so busy that I never worked for the Broadway Department Store again. I worked at Desmonds two days a week, and a woman named Mary Webb Davis became my agent. She was one of the best and most respected agents in the business. Her agency kept me busy working for many of the top photographers of the era, such as Tom Kelly, John Engstead and Richard Avedon.

One of my early jobs that I remember as being lots of fun was posing with Jimmy Durante for a record cover. We sat on a piano bench and he entertained by playing songs and singing. He would look at my nose and say, "Ah cha cha what a snozola, what a snozola."

Usually the Screen Children's Guild just called kids for extra work. But because there was always a demand for smaller children, we received a phone call to go to the American Legion Hall near the Hollywood Bowl. When we got there, we found a director and producer of a live TV show. The show was called the *NBC All Star Review*, and a group of comedians alternated each week as the guest host. One of these comedians was the great Ed Wynn.

First the director and producer went down the line of more than twenty kids in the four- to five-year-old range. They found a little boy who looked like Groucho Marx. They liked this kid a lot and wanted him to say the lines they gave him. He probably would have been just right for the part, but try as he might, he couldn't say his lines. As the director worked with the Groucho Marx look-alike, Ed Wynn went quietly down the line asking the other kids to say his lines. I was the next to the last one. When Ed Wynn got to me and asked me to repeat the line, "I'm the toughest hombre in these here parts," I said it back to him and a big smile came across his face. He called to the director and producer, still working with the other little boy, and said, "Come on down here, I found a kid who can say the line." He talked to me a while, and told me I had the part. At age two and a half, I was about to launch my acting career on the *NBC All Star Review* in front of a live audience.

They gave me a script for a cowboy saloon scene all done with kids. The lines were, "Step aside, Partner! Set 'em up. I'm the toughest hombre in these here parts." This was live TV, so there was no room for error. My mom recalls that we came home with the script. I sat at my little desk, and she tried to teach me the lines. But I was stubborn. She tried and tried, but couldn't get me to say the lines even once.

We were supposed to go back to the American Legion Hall again in a couple of days. My mother was so dismayed that she wanted to call the show and cancel, but she couldn't reach them. She had no choice but to take me to the Hall and try to explain to the director that I didn't know my lines and they should get someone else.

But she never had a chance to tell anyone. As soon as we walked in, they said, "OK, kids! Come over here!" Something just clicked, because I walked right over and knew all my lines. I marched right in there and did them perfectly. The older kids didn't know their lines as well as I did.

So my acting debut turned out to be what my mother thought would be the end of my brief career. It also turned out to be a big hit. I was noticed in *Daily Variety* as the kid in diapers with the ten gallon hat who drew such big laughs.

The saloon scene was a commercial for Pet Milk, the sponsor of the show. I walked through the swinging doors of the saloon with diapers on. I also had on cowboy boots, a two-gun holster, and a big ten gallon hat. I came in with my six guns blazing. I yelled, "Step aside partners!" Then I walked to the bar and pounded my fists, then demanded "Set 'em up." Ed Wynn asked, "Who are you?" I said, "I'm the toughest hombre in these here parts!" Ed Wynn sets up a baby bottle, and I drink it, nipple and all. People were just roaring.

Because I was so young, I don't remember too much about Ed Wynn. He was funny, but he was also a little scary. He had been a big vaudeville star, and he was doing all this crazy stuff that I know now was part of his act. He was so different from anyone I had seen before—very animated, with his funny hat and long checkered coat.

During the fifth year of *Leave It to Beaver*, Ed Wynn was doing a *GE Theater* on the Universal lot. I went to his set and visited him. He said he remembered me and the cowboy skit well. He had a photographer on the set take a picture of the two of us. I'm really happy I spent that time with him and have the photograph because that was one of his last performances before he died.

My life, like I guess a lot of people's, seems to be full of coincidences. When I was about four, I landed my first job on a major studio lot. It was MGM and the movie was *Men of the Fighting Lady*. I played Keenan Wynn's son. So, I did my first TV show with Ed Wynn and my first movie with his son Keenan.

I was suddenly on a roll. Between commercials, fashion shows, and television, I was one busy kid. I was also very lucky. The big movie studios were being assaulted by the advent of TV. The old studio system may have started to fade, but TV was on the rise. Live TV offered me lots of valuable experience, especially as a child actor, and kept me working regularly. Usually someone would ask one of the photographers if they knew any little boys who took direction well and were easy to work with. That is basically how I got my parts. I was always very lucky that way. I'd be doing one part, someone would see me, and hire me for something else.

I was able to work with some the most talented people in the industry. Remember too, that this was live TV and people were very nervous about that. People today think that shows were always taped as they are now. Live TV was so much different. Once you walked on stage, every little move you made was captured by the audience. If you panicked in front of the audience there was no editing it out later.

One show where total panic reigned was the *Spike Jones Show*. Jim Backus and his wife Penny were there. Spike Jones would come out and the band would play its madcap music, and I'd walk out with a sign and say, "Time for a commercial!" The directors would tell me what to do. I'd rehearse it a couple of times, and then I'd just do it. It was natural to some degree. Although I was only three years old, I had done lots of live fashion shows, and nothing bad had ever happened. I knew if you walked out in front of people and they applauded and told you what a good job you did, there wasn't very much to be afraid of. So it was an easy breakthrough from fashion shows to live TV.

My mother, however, tells of an incident which was a little different. It was a live *Matinee Theater* with Arthur Hiller, a budding director fresh from Canada. He entrusted me with a rather significant role being that I was only about five. We rehearsed in a building in Hollywood for three days and then went for the taping to NBC studios in Burbank. The Burbank studio was new; it had just opened. We arrived early in the morning and did one rehearsal. Then everything was set and we did a dress rehearsal. The actors all did well with their dialogue, but the set was catastrophic and just didn't work. The scene was between a burglar, dressed as Santa, and a little boy in some kind of a child's bed. The producer and director were frantic and changed the bed, and then had to change a few of my lines. The time between the dress rehearsal and the actual live broadcast was only about an hour. Arthur Hiller had just enough time to go over the new lines with me and put me in the scene before it was time to start. I said all the changes perfectly, and everyone was elated and made a big fuss over me. As we were driving home, I said to my mother, "Next time I do a show, don't tell me when it's the real show. Tell me it's the dress rehearsal." "Why, did you get nervous?" my mother asked. "No," I replied, "but my stomach got jumpy."

Arthur Hiller went on to direct *The Addams Family* on TV, and major motion pictures like *The Out of Towners*, *Love Story*, and *Plaza Suite*.

I also worked with Ray Bolger when I was pretty young, but I'm glad I can still remember because it was a lot of fun. It was called *The Ray Bolger Show* and was done at the original Desilu Studio. The story was about two orphans, a sister, and her little brother. They've run away from the orphanage and are hiding in an empty movie theater. The girl is doing something and has stationed her little brother to signal if anyone comes. He sees Ray Bolger and goes "dum-de-dum-dum," the *Dragnet* theme. They're soon discovered and Ray Bolger finds out their story and that they're very much afraid. He talks to them and then tells them that when he's afraid he whistles. Then he sings, "Whenever I feel afraid . . . I whistle a little tune, and no one ever knows I'm afraid." He also did a little dancing. I was very impressed because I knew he was the Scarecrow in *The Wizard of Oz* and I remember how much I loved him.

Even though I was so young, I was a veteran of live TV and so worked often when they needed a small boy. At CBS I worked on the *Red Skelton Show*. It was a circus skit with a few youngsters and I recall Red Skelton as being funny and nice.

I also remember working live with Jerry Lewis. It was NBC's *Colgate Comedy Hour* taped at Fred Murry's Blackouts Theater on Vine Street in Hollywood. The skit took place in an orphanage with about four little boys lined up with a husband and wife going down the line to see which one they wanted to adopt. Jerry Lewis was at the end of the line because he had been there for years and no one wanted to adopt him. So in rehearsal he moved in beside each little boy and did his antics, trying to be cute and have them choose him. Well, the other boys were a little older than I was and they thought Jerry Lewis was very funny, so they laughed at him. This didn't work at all, so when the live show came he did all his tricks just with me. And the more I kept a straight face the more ridiculous he became. Afterward, I confided to my mother that the reason I didn't laugh was because I didn't think he was funny.

I did another live show at CBS, though I can't remember

its name, and an incident occurred during the live broadcast that stands out in my mind. I was supposed to run into the arms of my father and then say several lines. The actor playing my father was an esteemed Broadway stage actor. The rehearsals went fine, but during the live show I tripped just before I got to his arms. He had the main lead in the show and I was only in the first scene. He had one of the stage crew come over and tell me not to leave after the show but wait because he wanted to talk to me. I felt bad. I thought he was going to scold me for tripping. To my surprise he told me how proud he was of me. He said I was a real trouper because I got up and carried on saying all my lines. Reminiscing about all these different events, I realize how genuinely nice show business people are. I'm glad I had these opportunities to be around them when I was a youngster.

When I was still very young and still living in Hollywood, we got a call to go to an old studio on Santa Monica Boulevard. It was fairly close to where we lived. When we got there it was for the *Ozzie and Harriet Show*. There were three little girls and three little boys. Ozzie selected me and a little girl and sent us right to makeup. It was a Halloween skit and I was made up as a pirate and the girl as something simple, maybe a witch. We never rehearsed. He just told us to come up and ring the doorbell and say, "trick or treat." He answered the door and when we said trick or treat he got candy and filled our little bags. No rehearsal. One take. That was it. In less than two hours, we were cast, made up, did the scene and released. These were the earliest years of the Nelson show. I have to say it was absolutely the most casual, laid-back job I ever did of course, I went home a happy chappy with a bag full of candy and an early start on Halloween.

Another star I had the privilege to work for was James Mason. He had written and was producing and directing a short Christmas story. His daughter, Portland, was Mary and I played Joseph. We worked for about three days in one of the old studios in the heart of Hollywood. One scene was with a real donkey which Portland sat on as I led her around looking for a place at the Inn. At this time, James and especially his wife, Pamela Ma-

son, were very big players in the Hollywood social scene. Just
about every week there was mention of them in Louella Parson
or Hedda Hopper's column. Often Portland was mentioned with
them and portrayed as very precocious and saying something
which came off as rather bratty. Well, it had to be just a lot of
hype because in reality Portland was a great little girl, unpreten-
tious and very likable. All the children in the cast were invited
to the Masons' Beverly Hills home to see the finished show. I
was also invited to birthday parties at their house. Portland was
always well behaved and just a really regular, nice kid.

James Mason also directed another film which was shot at
the 20th-Century Fox lot. He cast me in a small role which gave
me my only opportunity to work at Fox studio.

Just before I went to work on *Leave It to Beaver*, I worked on
a United Ways production with Frank Sinatra. It was while he
was filming the musical *Pal Joey* with Rita Hayworth and Kim
Novack. My mother was really concerned because Frank Sinatra
had a rough reputation. We were waiting anxiously on the set
with all the workers. Finally, he showed up and were we surprised. He was rough all right, but only with the big guys. He
was always nice to the little guys and the set workers. He just
fought the big guys. We've liked him ever since.

Each time I modeled or did a photo shoot, it led to more
jobs. Many times when I was called as an extra I ended up getting a major part. I did lots of television work, both live and
taped. I had a nice part on *Matinee Theater* with Cloris Leachman.
At the time, she was a young actress just getting started. Years
later, in 1971, she won a Best Supporting Oscar for her great
work in Peter Bogdonovich's *The Last Picture Show*.

Then I had a couple of shots with the *Lux Video Theater*. On
April 28, 1955, I did *The Great McGinty*, Lux's version of Preston
Sturges' 1940 biting satire of political corruption. Brian Donlevy
recreated his film role of Daniel J. McGinty, a bum who becomes
involved in politics. Jeri Weil and I played the two children.

In March 1956, I was in a very nice production of The Screen
Actor's Playhouse called *It's a Most Unusual Day* with Fred
MacMurray, soon to be the star of TV's *My Three Sons*. It featured
the songs of songwriter Jimmy McHugh. The production re-

ceived wonderful reviews and included such Jimmy McHugh standards as "I Can't Give You Anything But Love" and "Sunny Side of the Street."

Movies also beckoned. Between 1954 and 1957 I had parts in six films. My first movie was called *This Is My Love* with Linda Darnell and Dan Dureya in 1954. My mother took me on the interview. They seemed to like me, and said they also needed a little girl because the script called for two kids to play the children of Faith Domergue. I was quick to tell them about my sister Susie, who was three years old at the time.

The next day, my mother brought Susie to the studio. They just loved her, and decided to use both of us in the movie. It was filmed at Republic Studios and I thought Susie stole the show. Like me she had also done lots of modeling for catalogues and fashion shows, so the camera didn't scare her.

This Is My Love was especially exciting for my mother because Linda Darnell had been her idol when she was in high school. My dad loved her too because she was so pretty. In fact, my mother still has a letter from Linda Darnell saying what nice kids Susie and I were, and what a tremendous woman she felt my mother was. Linda Darnell was one of the top leading ladies of the 1940s, starring in such films as *The Mark of Zorro, My Darling Clementine, Forever Amber*, and *A Letter to Three Wives*. We were all very saddened to hear she died in a fire in 1965 while visiting a friend. She had fallen asleep in a chair with a lit cigarette.

After we finished *This Is My Love*, one of the local papers had a picture of Susie and me, lauding us as "the next Barrymores"—a pretty far stretch I'd have to say.

In *This Is My Love*, Susie had a line, "Don't take her appendix out! She already had her appendix out!" But she couldn't say "appendix," so I helped her out. When she was four years old she had her tonsils and adenoids removed, and it really helped her speech. We still laugh about this today. Susie always says that she rode my coattails well. When I was working, people would see Susie and say they could use a little girl for this or that part. But the truth is that she had a bundle of ability in her own right. She was a good little actress and was cute as a button. And full of mischief. Had she wanted to continue in the business she might have had a successful career as a child actress. But it was never that important to her.

One of my favorite Susie stories involved a party at Chasens. Shortly after the *Leave It to Beaver* pilot, and right before we started the series, she was sitting at the bar at Chasens. Of course Chasens was one of the marquee restaurants in Los Angeles. Because Susie was so adorable, people were buying her Shirley Temples left and right, and after six or seven drinks she couldn't wait any longer and wet her pants. The red velvet bar stool at Chasens was so high that it seems she couldn't get off and run to the bathroom.

Another time, during *Beaver*, we all went to Hawaii. I had to make appearances and work. Susie just had a great time. She met some sailors on the beach, and whenever the bill came my eight-year-old sister would sign for it. Everything was signed, "Susie Mathers." On the last day, my dad looked through the charges. We were there for about two weeks, but he had put just a few things on the charge himself. All the rest were these "Susie Mathers" signatures. Boy did she get into trouble for that.

Susie had a terrible crush on Tony Dow. On the plane ride to Hawaii, she jumped in the seat right next to him. He turned to his mom and said, "Get her away from me. I'm not sitting by her for five hours!" Our publicist, a real nice fellow by the name of Sam, rescued Tony. "Susie, here you can sit by me," he said quite gallantly. At get-togethers, Susie still gives Tony a hard time about it today.

My biggest break came in 1954 on the first hour-long production of *Lux Video Theater*. After a score of years on CBS with radio and TV, Lever Brothers, who sponsored the show, doubled its former running time from thirty minutes to an hour. The production was *To Each His Own*. The 1946 movie won an Academy Award for actress Olivia de Havilland. Aired on the *Lux Video Theater* on August 26, 1954, Dorothy McGuire recreated Olivia de Havilland's role. Gene Barry—who would later become a big TV star with shows like *Bat Masterson* and *Burke's Law*—played her son.

The story is a three-hanky tearjerker about an unwed mother who fights to win back her son. I played the little boy who grows up to be the Gene Barry character. Again, it was a matter of my being in the right place at the right time. Because the part called for a little boy with brown eyes to match the eyes of Gene Barry, I hadn't gone on the original interview. But the little boy they had in mind got sick at the last moment, and they were desperate because there were just a few more rehearsals and time was running short. Buzz Kulik, who later directed such TV gems as *Sergeant Ryker* and *Brian's Song*, asked me to recite the Pledge of Allegiance. That was all, nothing more! I must have recited it better than the other kids because I got the part. Kulik showed a lot of confidence in me—there were a number of lines and not much time to learn them.

Because it was live TV, the actors were running back and forth changing costumes backstage, with little modesty. I was only six years old, and was really shocked seeing people scurrying about and jumping behind little screens to change their clothes. This was blocked from the audience, but completely visible to me.

Because my character grew up to be the Gene Berry character, I was only in the beginning of the production. After my part was done I became very thirsty. But the water fountain was on the other side of the sound stage, and you had to be careful not to make any noise. I was wearing a little sleeper suit. There was a man sitting behind the glass screen who kept looking at me. He was pointing toward the water fountain. He could see my hesitation, and he motioned as if to encourage me to get that drink of water. I looked over at my mother, and she was motioning me to stay put. She was afraid I would make a disturbance, and live TV made it a pretty daring risk indeed. I decided to go for it anyway, heeding the advice of the man behind the glass. So I moved gingerly across the room, taking great care not to hit anything or to knock anything over. The man behind the glass kept watching me, watching my every move with a very serious look on his face.

I had no idea that the man behind the glass was the great director Alfred Hitchcock. I didn't even know who Alfred Hitchcock was. He was on the show that night to do an interview with James Mason who was hosting *Lux Video Theater*, and to plug his upcoming movie *Rear Window*.

We thought nothing more of the episode until a few days later when a driver came to the house quite unexpectedly to deliver a script. There was a note attached that read, "Mrs. Mathers, please have your son learn these lines. He will be called in for an interview." It was signed "Alfred Hitchcock." Hitchcock was casting for a new project. The film was *The Trouble with Harry*, and it was his first excursion into the realm of black comedy. He had me in mind for the role of Arnie Rogers. My mother in the film was a twenty-two-year-old actress, fresh from the Broadway musical stage, named Shirley MacLaine.

chapter 4
Oh, Hello, Mr. Mathers

The Trouble with Harry was my first work with Jerry. But he was a pro. He was a pro when he was five or six years old. Other than Jerry, Shirley MacLaine was an absolute revelation in that picture, and so kookie and delightful. She and Jerry, I think, were the finds in that picture. The rest of us all worked with some degree of success. It was a joyous experience.
—*John Forsythe*

When Hitchcock's note arrived it said only that I should read the script and be prepared to come in for an interview. No specific time or date was indicated. So life went on as usual.

The little girl down the street was having a birthday party one day. She took us all to the movies, then later we were supposed to go for lunch. Of course that was the day my parents got a call from Paramount Studios saying that Alfred Hitchcock wanted to see me immediately. In other words, right now! My dad got in the car, rushed to the movie theater, picked me up, and drove me to the studio. When I got to Paramount for my meeting with Hitchcock, I was starved, and even a little miffed because I hadn't been able to stay at the party with my friends.

What happened next was bizarre. When we arrived, Hitchcock was eating his lunch. He had four or five waiters serving him from these huge silver trays. One waiter appeared with a large tray. He opened it and there was this huge piece of meat. Hitchcock cut a piece of meat, just a single piece, put it on his plate, and took a bite—just one bite. Then the waiter closed the tray and wheeled it away. A second waiter came in with an entirely different tray. He uncovered it, and Hitchcock took a piece of the offering. He took just one bite again. Once more the waiter closed the tray and wheeled it away. He followed this same routine with the third, fourth, and fifth tray, each time just taking a single bite of the dish inside, then having the waiter wheel the tray away. All this time I was salivating, and thinking what a rich man he must be eating from these huge silver trays.

I'm sure Hitchcock had made up his mind about me long before the interview because I got the part with very little effort. The next thing I knew my mother said we were going to Stowe, Vermont, to film the movie. My grandmother, who lived with us at the time, would watch Susie while my dad was at work.

It was the first time I was ever on an airplane. We boarded one of those big four engine Convairs in Los Angeles, and arrived in New York with little trouble. But in New York we picked up a little DC 9, and I have never forgotten the ordeal to this day. It was a horrible flight. We couldn't land when we were supposed to. Everyone got airsick. There was a man sitting across the aisle from us, a handsome man in his early thirties who was very helpful to my mother and me. He was so nice and sweet to us, in fact, that my mother was sure he was a doctor. But he wasn't a doctor, he was actor John Forsythe, and he was slated to play the male lead in the movie, an idealistic artist named Sam Marlow.

Alfred Hitchcock was the movies' acknowledged master of suspense. He had been directing movies in England since 1926, with a long list of outstanding credits before arriving in Hollywood in 1940. Once here, he made a big name for himself directing stylish crime thrillers like *Foreign Correspondent* (1940), *Lifeboat* (1943), *Spellbound* (1945), *Strangers on a Train* (1951), and *Dial M for Murder* (1954). But *The Trouble with Harry* was entirely his baby. It was the first film he produced as well as directed. Always employing his own special combination of suspense and impudence, this was his first excursion into black comedy, and a truly innovative venture.

The Trouble with Harry was based on Jack Trevor Story's

novel about a corpse that a group of Vermont villagers keep burying and digging up again for their own reasons. It always remained one of Hitchcock's favorites among his own films. And it was absolutely a fun-filled time for me.

We had an outstanding cast. I've already mentioned John Forsythe, the actor who was so nice to us on that terrible plane ride. He was a veteran of many films, including *Destination Tokyo*, *Madam X*, and *Escape from Fort Bravo*. He became better known in the late 1950s for the TV series *Bachelor Father*, then as the voice of Charlie in the popular series, *Charlie's Angels*, and later for his role on *Dynasty*.

I probably spent more time with him than anyone else on the set. He was like a surrogate father to me. He would take time to play catch, throw me a ball, and show me lots of other things. Funny how after so many years you can recall a specific incident or two. Sometimes it's the little things that leave the largest imprint. Once, I asked John Forsythe why I couldn't throw a snowball very well. He put his arm around my shoulder like a pal and told me that if I put a rock in the center and built the snow around it, I could hit a tree at ten and twenty yards. I said something like "Holy Smokes! OK!" Then he added that I should throw only at trees, never at people or animals.

Another person who was very nice to me on the set was Edmund Gwenn. He insisted that I join him in his photo ops. An outstanding character actor, he is best remembered for his Oscar-winning role as Santa Claus in the 1948 film classic, *Miracle on 34th Street*. Two years later he was nominated again for a Best Supporting Oscar, this time as an elderly counterfeiter in the movie *Mr. 880*. If John Forsythe was like a surrogate dad to me on the set, Edmund Gwenn was my surrogate grandfather. He seemed to delight in having me around.

People ask me to compare Ed Wynn with Edmund Gwenn. Maybe because their names have a similar ring, and because I worked with both men when I was still a little boy. They were totally different. As I said earlier, I found Ed Wynn a little on the scary side because of his long jacket and funny clothes. Edmund Gwenn I remember as a nice, calm person. When we were going through the Mathers family picture albums not long ago, there were more pictures of me with Edmund Gwenn than with anyone else in the cast.

The Trouble with Harry marked the screen debut of Shirley MacLaine. She had been performing on Broadway as Carol Haney's understudy in the hit musical *The Pajama Game*. When Carol Haney injured her leg, Shirley MacLaine, a superb dancer, took over. Something about her so impressed Hitchcock that he cast her as Jeniffer Rogers in *The Trouble with Harry*.

I played her five-year-old son Arnie Rogers. It's simply amazing how much we actually looked alike back then. Rent the video and take a close look. It's almost uncanny. We could really have been mother and son. As far as I know, however, this was not Hitchcock's original intention. It was just fortuitous and added even more authenticity to both our roles.

I didn't see Shirley MacLaine again until I was doing another film at Paramount. She was making the Academy Award–winning *Around the World in 80 Days*. She played the princess and she was still in costume when I saw her at the commissary. She recognized me and said, "Jerry, how nice to see you!" But it felt strange to me because I hadn't remembered her all dressed up like that. As a kid, you picture a person just one way, and I couldn't easily understand her transition from New England mother to exotic princess in just a year's time.

Of course, Shirley MacLaine became an Oscar-winning actress, a controversial best-selling author, and one of the industry's acknowledged superstars. But I bet most people don't have any idea that her film debut was as my mother in *The Trouble with Harry* nearly forty-five years ago.

When you work on location, you tend to get a lot closer than when you work on the studio lot. When you work at a studio you really don't get to know people that well. Everybody goes home at the end of the work day. But when you are in a community, especially one like Stowe, Vermont, where there aren't many things to do socially, the company tends to go out for dinner together. In Stowe, the local community went all out for us. I still love blueberry muffins because many of the local ladies picked wild blueberries and made muffins for us. In fact, they had a contest to see which one's Hitchcock would pick to eat.

When we arrived in Stowe, we were put up at a little ski resort. The whole reason for going there was the beautiful autumn leaves of Vermont—breathtaking is perhaps a better word. For about two or three weeks the cast stayed in Stowe doing nothing because Hitchcock wasn't completely satisfied with the depth of the colors. Every day the good people of Stowe would assure him that the leaves would be more bright and colorful the next day. "Just wait one more day," they told him almost every day. Meanwhile, Hitchcock kept his crew and cast on salary. Finally, he had what he wanted with the leaves and told us we would begin production the next day. But that very night a huge wind- and rainstorm knocked all the leaves off every tree. Here we had been waiting for weeks for the leaves to turn the proper shade, now there were no leaves at all. Hitchcock was in a real dilemma.

Well, there happened to be trees in a section of Germany where leaves stayed basically the same autumn colors all year long. So Hitchcock sent two cargo planes to Germany. They cut down the limbs and branches and flew them back to Stowe, Vermont, in time to start production. The magnificent colors and leaves you see in the film were actually imported from Europe.

I almost begin the picture. I'm strolling through the woods carrying a toy gun, when I stumble upon a dead body. I turn around and run to tell my mother. But she and the other main characters, far from viewing the scenario with dismay and horror, take a whimsical attitude toward the corpse. Each has a likely reason for wishing the state of the deceased to remain concealed.

Edmund Gwenn plays a kindly but crusty old fellow named Captain Wilkes. He thinks he shot Harry (the corpse) while hunting rabbits on the hill. Mrs. Gravely, an old maid played by Mildred Natwick, thinks she's responsible because she conked Harry on the head when he was ruthlessly trying to attack her. Jeniffer Rogers (my mom) was actually married to Harry and bopped him on the head with a milk bottle when he appeared at our house. She is quite relieved to have him dead. All the while, the debonair artist, played by John Forsythe, gets lots of innocent amusement from moving the corpse and helping his friends. There is a certain hilarity to *The Trouble with Harry*, quite unique among Hitchcock's films.

Hitchcock wanted to dress me like a little English boy. That's why I am wearing shorts and a little T-shirt. It was cold that time of year in Vermont, but I'm wearing shorts and my hair is in bangs. This was more of an English look for a little boy than an American look.

I still like to watch this movie, especially the crisp ironic dialogue, and the accent on humor.

There is a scene where I trade my dead rabbit to John Forsythe for his live frog. I tell him that I got the best of the deal because dead rabbits don't eat. The rabbit wasn't dead of course. What I was really holding in my hand was a stuffed toy rabbit. It was a difficult scene because they changed the dialogue the night before, and they were afraid I might not be able to learn my new lines. It went something like "Why is tomorrow yesterday, Mr. Marlow, if yesterday is today?" But it went well, and John Forsythe and I had a lot of fun with the scene.

Alfred Hitchcock never really talked to actors much. He was very aloof, and he had the reputation of not liking actors. Some people made the mistake of thinking that his aloofness meant that he wasn't paying attention to anyone on the set. Quite the opposite was true. Hitchcock knew every little thing that was going on around him. In fact, he had an obsession for detail and perfection. If someone was not doing what they were supposed to be doing, he would know it. He could intimidate people and he often did.

When I was doing *Leave It to Beaver* and shooting at Universal, Hitchcock was making *The Birds*. Susie went on an interview for the part of the little girl—the part Veronica Cartwright played in the movie. Veronica Cartwright, like her sister Angela, went on to a successful career in film and TV. She is still a working actress. Veronica played Violet Rutherford on *Leave It to Beaver*, and she had the distinction of giving the Beaver his first real TV kiss.

As Susie tells it, she went in for the interview and Alfred Hitchcock was lying on the couch in his big office at Universal. He didn't get up. He proceeded to ask Susie a lot of "weird things." She thought he was very scary. But he never really phased me. Maybe because I was so young. Or maybe it was because I was used to working with big stars since I was a toddler, and I had lots of experience doing live TV.

After I finished *The Trouble with Harry*, Alfred Hitchcock came to the studio to do *Alfred Hitchcock Presents*. In fact, one of the episodes of *Alfred Hitchcock Presents* was actually shot in the *Leave It to Beaver* living room.

He would come to the studio for one day and do five or six different introductions for episodes, then wait another two weeks before he came again. I would be playing on the lot with the other kids, and he'd sail in with his chauffeur-driven Rolls Royce. As he'd drive by, he'd have his chauffeur stop the car. He'd make it a point to roll down the window and say, "Oh, Hello, Mr. Mathers!" He'd say, "How are you doing today! I'm here to do my show. Is everything all right? Are you having a good time playing? I just wanted to say 'Hi!' " Then he would say, "Goodbye, Mr. Mathers," close the window, and drive away. I thought it was pretty funny. He was the first person ever to call me Mr. Mathers. Most people at the time called me Jerry or Beaver.

The critics were only lukewarm to *The Trouble with Harry*, although today it scores lots of points and is considered a classic by some. Because it was a black comedy in general, and an English black comedy in particular, it was a bit ahead of its time. It never received the same kind of success here in the United States as most of Hitchcock's other films. John Forsythe has pointed out that we don't have the same attitudes about murder, comedy murder, and comedy deaths that the Europeans have. Their attitudes toward black comedy are more sophisticated. And in 1955, the ribald nature of digging up a body, then hiding it, then digging it up again, didn't sit particularly well with many Americans.

Nevertheless, the picture was a success. It made a good deal of money abroad (the movie ran in Paris for well over a year). In fact, Barabara Billingsly told me not long ago that she first saw *The Trouble with Harry* in 1956 while in Paris with her husband. Little did she think that just a short time later our careers and our lives would become mutually entwined and forever linked.

My time spent making *The Trouble with Harry* is full of great memories. I'll never forget those huge silver trays and Mr. Hitchcock's peculiar culinary habits; nor how hungry I was and how I returned to the birthday party just as soon as my interview was over. I have never forgotten the majestic beauty of rural Vermont, and the vivid allure of those orange leaves. During my free time I'd walk along all those picturesque roads, lunching at little quaint inns, buying maple syrup, and eating blueberry muffins. Nor will I forget a particularly pleasant evening when there were barrels with fires set inside them, and how we sent out for frankfurters and roasted them by the campfire. This was supposed to be most unlike Mr. Hitchcock.

At about the same time, back in Hollywood, two gifted writers by the names of Joe Connelly and Bob Mosher were in the planning stages of a new TV series to enhance their already distinguished list of writing credits. What they had in mind was to show the amusing and often contradictory world of adults through the eyes of two boys. The proposed show was yet untitled, and there was still lots of work to do.

But before I met Connelly and Mosher, I worked with Bob Hope in two movies. He is a great comedian, and one of the most tremendous performers show business has ever known. His work on behalf of America's servicemen is legendary. In our family he holds a very special place. During the filming of *The Seven Little Foys* for Paramount, Bob Hope saved my life.

chapter 5

Thanks for the Memory

My mom would always say when we went out on an interview that we shouldn't tell anybody because we never knew what might happen. I think Jerry got every part he went out for. And he never really cared either.

—*Susie Mathers McSweeney*

T he song "Thanks for the Memory" has forever been associated with Bob Hope, since it first appeared as the Oscar-winning song in the movie *The Big Broadcast of 1938*. For seven decades he has delighted audiences with his deft comedy, self-deprecating wit, and superb showmanship. His Armed Forces Benefit Shows have earned the gratitude of four generations of American servicemen. Courage was not a commodity Bob Hope ever lacked. He literally performed under fire.

When I was seven years old, I had an opportunity to see Hope's courage in action. Few people have left as lasting an imprint on my life as Bob Hope.

My mother has often said that if she knew then what she was soon to find out she would never have let me do *The Seven Little Foys*. The movie is the story of entertainer/comedian Eddie Foy, who built his famous vaudeville act around himself and his seven children after his wife died. Directed by Melville Shavelson (*Cast a Giant Shadow*, *The Five Pennies*, and *Houseboat*), the film's high point was the appearance of James Cagney re-creating his role of

George M. Cohan and dancing on a tabletop with Bob Hope to the strains of "Mary" and "Yankee Doodle Boy."

In the picture I played Brian Foy as a little boy. I had to be extremely bratty. Once again, I was not originally slated for the picture. I kept getting called back and called back, but as time passed I had not heard anything definite. We received word that someone else got the part of the youngest boy. Naturally, I was disappointed. What actually happened was that the Foy family—actually the oldest daughter—was the technical advisor, and she decided that the kids should look like the people they were playing in the movie. That's why I was passed over.

Then came another call from the studio. We were told to come back one more time. It seems that Melville Shavelson, the director, Jack Rose, the producer, and the Foy family in general, were very impressed with me. So they wrote me in for a special part—that of Brian Foy as a very young boy. In the scene, Bob Hope brings me to the theater. I'm a spoiled little guy with a stick of licorice in my mouth. I'm pouting and screaming that I don't want to go into the theater with my father. (I'd never played such an annoying kid before.)

I had never had licorice before, but fortunately, I just loved it. In fact, I still do. So to please me, the crew bought me these huge sticks of licorice. The prop man said I should eat all that I wanted, and that's just what I did. I guess the prop man lived to regret his words because he later said that I ate thirty sticks of licorice. The story was picked up by the *Los Angeles Mirror News* in its issue of May 31, 1955, under the banner "Moppet Polished Off Thirty Licorice Sticks":

Little Jerry Mathers put a dent in the budget of Paramount's *The Seven Little Foys*. In a scene with Bob Hope, Jerry, who plays Bryan Foy at age five, is seen eating licorice. Prop man Earl Olin said he could have all the candy that was left. When Jerry came to collect there wasn't any. In two days he had consumed thirty sticks of licorice.

There is a dramatic scene in the picture that re-created the tragic Iroquois Theater Fire in Chicago. Eddie Foy was performing at the Iroquois Theater when the fire broke out. He sang and danced, and tried to keep people from trampling each other. He was the hero of the day.

Bryan Foy was not actually in the real Iroquois Theater fire. Remember they had written the part into the film especially for me, and it almost cost me my life. The fire scene has Bryan Foy sitting up in the balcony on a swing. When the fire started, there was supposed to be a stuntman doubling for Bob Hope. The stuntman was supposed to climb up, grab me, and bring me down. That's what you actually see in the movie. But that was shot the following day.

What originally happened was that they put too much gasoline on all the curtains, and suddenly the curtains burst into flames. Of course no one expected real flames. I was sitting there waiting for someone to get me, but there was no stuntman. It was Bob Hope who climbed up the ladder, grabbed me, and got me out of there. Otherwise, I probably would have burned to death or suffocated from all the smoke.

I was very young and in a state of panic. Being so young, I don't remember every detail. My mother was on the set and was petrified with fear. She remembers everything and reminds me of the details: "I read the script and I knew there is a fire. But little did I know that they used actual fire. I thought they did it with lights, and that they just put the lights around to make it look like it's burning. Well, they did this scene with actual fire. There was always a stuntman for Bob Hope, and there were a lot of extras that were in costume. They had taken the ladder away, just a little bit away, and Jerry was up there in a swing. They didn't do it right and there was terrible smoke. I couldn't believe it. The stuntman was right below, and he pushed out the door. He left Jerry up there alone. Bob Hope ran in, pushed the ladder, and climbed up and saved Jerry. He's a brave man."

What my mother neglected to say was that we shot the scene again the next day. I'd be a liar if I didn't say I was scared but I managed to do it well. Bob Hope must have been impressed with me, because he personally cast me in his next picture—*That Certain Feeling*. The movie was co-produced, co-directed, and co-written by Norman Panama and Melvin Frank, who were Bob

Hope's personal writers. Their directing credits, individually and combined, include *The Court Jester* with Danny Kaye, Neil Simon's *The Prisoner of Second Avenue* with Jack Lemmon and Anne Bancroft, and *A Touch of Class*, which won a Best Actress Oscar in 1973 for Glenda Jackson.

Panama and Frank were two of the industry's top writers turned directors, with a real flare for comedy. It was a great cast: Bob Hope, Eva Marie Saint, George Sanders, and Pearl Bailey. It was a fun film that still plays well today. But because Panama and Frank were both writers, they took an enormous amount of takes. Either one or the other wasn't satisfied. If Panama wanted to do it one way, Frank would want to do it another way, and vice versa. So there might be twenty-five to fifty takes of the same scene.

The opening night at the Paramount Theater was really something. There were lots of people. Bob Hope and Pearl Bailey appeared for four performances on the stage. They were introduced at the successive shows by TV personalities Dave Garroway, Hy Gardner, Faye Emerson, Edward R. Murrow, and Louis Bellson and His Orchestra.

In the movie, I played an adopted orphan boy named Norman Taylor. Bob Hope was a neurotic cartoonist named Francis K. Digman, who was divorced from his wife Dunreath Henry (played by Eva Marie Saint). The character was loosely based on Al Capp, who played himself in the movie.

There were some great comedy scenes in the film. It was the first comedy fling for Eva Marie Saint, who two years earlier in 1954 won an Academy Award for Best Supporting Actress in her film debut *On the Waterfront*. In the movie Eva Marie Saint finds her ex-husband (Bob Hope) down on his luck. She is engaged to a rather pompous fellow named Larry Larkin (played by George Sanders), and she convinces him to give Bob Hope a job. Meanwhile, she and Bob Hope fall in love all over again.

One hilarious scene has Bob Hope and Eva Marie Saint decked out in Chinese costumes inside a penthouse apartment, bellowing out the title song. At the end of a series of shenanigans, it all ends in a farcical splurge of domestic confusion on Edward R. Murrow's *Person to Person* TV show. Murrow comes to their house to do a segment of his show. I have an old scruffy dog, and when the time comes for the big TV interview there is total mayhem. The dog gets out and runs around loose, while everyone is chasing him. It's a very funny scene that required lots of takes.

One of the odd things that happened involved Pearl Bailey, who played the maid. I was always kind of shy one-on-one and I was raised to be polite, so when the adults didn't come over to me I usually didn't go over to them. At the end of the movie we were all getting ready to say goodbye. I went over to Pearl Bailey, gave her a big hug, kissed her, said goodbye, and told her how nice it was to work with her. She said, "Oh, you're such a nice boy. And I didn't think you liked me because I was 'colored.' " I didn't understand it at all, because that never crossed my mind. I wasn't brought up that way. She was an adult, and I was always taught that unless an adult talks to you, you didn't just go up and talk to them.

After we did *The Seven Little Foys*, Bob Hope gave me a watch. It was inscribed simply, "To Jerry. From Bob Hope!" I was very surprised when he gave me the watch. It was Christmas, but I never expected a gift like this. He was such a big star, but you never would have known that by the way he acted. His son Kelly also had a part in one scene, so for one day we went to school together.

Bob Hope and I have crossed paths over the years at different times, and we always say "hello." He will always remain a hero to me. Not just for his great work with the Armed Forces, or for being an outstanding American. Not only for his wonderful contribution to our industry and for all the laughter and mirth he engendered. But for saving my life with an act of great courage. So quite officially, and for the record, Bob, thanks for all those wonderful memories and marvelous moments you have given all of us for so very long.

There were two more films during my pre-Beaver days that warrant mention. The first was a taut little thriller called *The Shadow on the Window*. It starred Phil Carey and Betty Garret, and was named the Best B Movie of 1956.

The last movie I made before *Leave It to Beaver* gave me the opportunity to work with one of the movie's great stars: Alan Ladd. The movie was *The Deep Six*, and it also starred William Bendix, James Whitmore, Efrem Zimbalist Jr., and Keenan Wynn, that fine character actor, and the son of Ed Wynn, who I first worked with on the *NBC All Star Review*.

I had always liked Alan Ladd, and his performance in *Shane*, one of my favorite Westerns, is simply a classic. In the 1940s, Ladd had been Paramount Pictures' most popular star, and *Shane* kept him at the pinnacle of his success. He left Paramount a short time later, and his career began to go downhill. He started fighting a battle with alcohol and pills, which eventually caused his death in 1964 at age fifty.

In *The Deep Six* Ladd played Alex Austin, a Naval ROTC officer with a Quaker background who was called to active duty after Pearl Harbor. It was a fun shoot because we went up to Monterey and Carmel, and a lot of the scenes were shot at Pebble Beach with its different panoramic views.

During a scene with Alan Ladd I had a line I just could not get right. It was "My dad is a sailor on the sailing ship Quency." I just could not get the line right. A real tongue twister! Then Alan Ladd, my hero, went beserk! "What the hell is wrong with this kid," he screamed. He stormed off to his dressing room to cool down for ten minutes. When he came back I read the line perfectly, but he could not get his own lines right. We had to do fourteen takes before he stopped making a mistake. I did not get angry and storm off to my dressing room, but I did not forget.

I had a scene with another little boy named Steve, and we were supposed to be annoying Alan Ladd because he was going out with our mother, played by Dianne Foster. We were down by the ocean fishing, and the director Rudolph Mate said, "When these kids come up here, what can we do that can be real annoying?" He wanted something that would make the scene work well.

I had this wet fish at the end of my line. Everybody was throwing different ideas around, so I stuck my two cents in. I said, "What if I hit him with the fish." Well, everybody just loved the idea. So that became the first comedy bit I ever wrote, and it was all for revenge! In the scene I go right up to Alan

Ladd, and when I am standing there with the fish at the end of the hook, I swing the slimy fish into his face. It took Rudolph Mate ten takes to get the scene right, so I got to hit Alan Ladd with that fish ten times. I remember loving each time that gooey fish hit him in the face. I had a hunch that Rudolph Mate and the crew loved it as much as I did.

I was the kind of kid who when someone asked, "Can you do this or that?" I would always say yes. So when I interviewed for *The Deep Six* and they asked me if I could ride a horse, my reply was simple: "Of course I can ride a horse. Anybody can ride a horse." After the fish scene, we were all supposed to go horseback riding. Because I had said I could ride horses, they probably figured that I was an accomplished rider. They had gotten four high-spirited quarter horses from a nearby ranch in Carmel.

We were riding along at a leisurely pace, when something spooked one of the horses. My horse and the other kid's horse just took off. I was riding a huge quarter horse, and it was out of control. I hit the branch of a tree and was knocked clear off the horse. Fortunately, I wasn't injured badly, though it was quite a scare.

Again much of what I remember and recall is just a snapshot because I was so young. When you're a child actor making movies and you're not working in a particular scene, you're either in school or away from the set. Making movies requires absolute quiet. So children tended to be isolated from the rest of the cast.

I remember Alan Ladd as rather short. He was not 5'2" or 5'3" as some of his detractors like to claim. Rather he was about 5'6" or 5'7", which still made it necessary for him to play some scenes on a box or an incline when squaring off with another man or playing a love scene with a taller woman.

But all this pales today. By the time *The Deep Six* hit the movie theaters in 1958, my life had taken a sudden turn. I was no longer just Jerry Mathers, child actor. I was now Beaver Cleaver, and I was among the most recognizable faces in the booming world of TV.

chapter 6

Here Come the Cleavers

Much of the success of Leave It to Beaver is that it's the type of show you can relate to as a family. They were very honest and believable with the scenes. I knew people who had kids like Tony and Jerry, and you could relate to them immediately. People who would say things like, "My kid did the same thing the other night." There was a natural quality about Jerry Mathers you rarely found in other young actors. It was a business for him, and he did it very well.
—*Earl Bellamy, Director*

By 1957 we were growing as a family. My sister Susie was already six years old, and my brother Jimmy was pushing two. We had moved into a large home in Canoga Park, and my mother and father would soon celebrate their tenth wedding anniversary.

By now I was a time-tested show business veteran. By the time I was eight, I had appeared before a camera in a professional capacity for nearly six years. And *The Trouble with Harry* finally made many people take notice of me as an actor. I had a new agent who kept busy lining me up with parts. But the one thing my parents were dead set against was my doing a series. I loved to work, but my mother reasoned that a series would not keep a kid like me very interested for very long. She felt that working day after day, any kid, not just me, would get just plain tired of it. So she refused to take me on any interview that might involve a series. And she was serious. One time the agent called to tell my mother about a new series with Jim Backus and Joan

Davis, and she wanted to know if I was available for an interview. But my mother held firm and wouldn't take me.

Then a short time later, my agent heard that they were casting for a new series that required a whole lot of kids, but they hadn't found anybody they liked. Employing a bit of a ruse, she called my mother but neglected to tell her the interview was for a series. Rather, she acted like it was only a week's work.

In a sense the agent was right. The casting call was for a pilot called *It's a Small World*, which they hoped might lead to a series. My mother took me to Republic (Revue) Studios. When we got there it was a cattle call for all sorts of parts, but the main two characters were to be two boys, ages six to fifteen, to play brothers in a middle America setting.

There were all kinds of kids in this little casting room. They started calling the kids up by age. When I went up they sent the other boys away. Shortly, a man came down with a script and said, "Mrs. Mathers, will you teach Jerry the lines? He says he learns his lines by his mother reading to him." The truth was that I had a very hard time reading. Although no one knew it at the time, I was struggling with dyslexia, which made reading very difficult. My mother and I went into another little room to learn the lines. When they called me up, they started calling up the older boys one by one. They were looking for good matches. With each reading they would eliminate one or two of the kids, maybe both.

I was called in for a couple of very extensive interviews, while others were slowly being weeded out. Finally I got a call for the big one. But there was a problem. I had a Cub Scout meeting that same day at 4 P.M. and did not want to miss it. I was far more excited about my Cub Scout meeting than I was about the interview. I wasn't too happy about it, but my mother said that we had put in a lot of time, and that it would be a shame to be down to the very last day and not get the job because of a Cub Scout meeting. My interview was set for about 3:30, so I wore my Cub Scout Uniform, badges and all, so I could go to the Cub Scout meeting directly after the interview. You can bet I was the only kid who showed up wearing his Cub Scout uniform.

We went to the second floor, and they took me into one room and my mother waited in another. Remember, we had no idea that I was interviewing for a series. But the cover was blown when a man came by from MCA and said to my mother, "Wow, this is going to be the best series. These writers are so great. They wrote the *Amos 'n' Andy* shows. They wrote for Bob Cummings. And they are going to do this new series, which is just great!"

The interviewing had been an interesting process. At the start, a casting director eliminates a large group who aren't suitable. Those who are left usually go through two layers of casting directors. By that time, Mr. Mosher and Mr. Connelly were able to watch those who had survived the cuts.

For the final interview, Mr. Connelly was ill, so I interviewed only with Mr. Mosher. But Mr. Connelly had been there for all the other interviews, so they had a good sheet on me. Mr. Mosher noticed that I kept looking at my watch, and asked me what was wrong. He had kids of his own, and he could see that I had always been polite, but here I was jumping all around.

He asked me again, "What's wrong? Don't you want to be here?" I said, "No, I want to be at my Cub Scout meeting!" He said, "You're in uniform!" I said, "Yeah, because I want to be at the Cub Scout meeting, and I'm going to miss it now because we've been waiting out here."

So he said, "Well, why don't you just go to your Cub Scout meeting?" I thought it was just great. I went running out the door, and my mom asked me what happened. I told her that he asked me if I had somewhere to go, and I told him I wanted to go to my Cub Scout meeting. My mother was dismayed. We had wasted all this time, she scolded. Now they'll think I'm not interested in their TV show and would rather go to my Cub Scout meeting. "They're right," I told her once again. "I'd rather be at my Cub Scout meeting!"

That night my dad was reading the *Herald Examiner*. I can see him now. He had just read an article that said there were thirty-four pilots being made for TV, and there were spots for only about three. He was sure that our pilot would never sell, so I might as well make the money as the next kid. At almost the same moment my agent called to say that I had gotten the part. I got it because they were looking for someone who was a real little boy; one who would be more interested in going to a Cub Scout meeting than doing a TV show.

It's a Small World appeared on as a *Heinz Studio '57* production on April 23, 1957. Back then, sponsors would subsidize a pilot for a show, and if they liked it they would front the series.

The original pilot had been lost until recently. Thirty years after the pilot aired we suddenly started looking for it. Everybody thought it had been called "Wally and the Beaver," and no one seemed to remember that it originally was aired on *Heinz Studio '57*. A senior vice president of Universal happened to be doing an inventory in a film vault at a Universal warehouse in Chicago when he saw Barbara Billingsly and my names listed on a 30-minute show called *It's a Small World*. He got the archivist to get the film and discovered that it was the original *Leave It to Beaver*.

The reason only Barbara and my names were listed was because the Ward and Wally characters were not played by Hugh Beaumont and Tony Dow in the original pilot. Ward was played by Casey Adams, and Wally was played by Paul Sullivan. Among future series regulars, Diane Brewster and Richard Deacon also appeared in the pilot.

We had one of the top TV directors at the helm—Earl Bellamy. Mr. Bellamy had risen through the ranks, starting as an office boy at Columbia Studios in 1935. He worked his way into production, then to second unit director, and then first assistant director. After working for a number of outstanding directors like George Cukor and Fred Zinnemann, he began directing on his own in 1954. In his heyday, he directed between 1,500 and 1,600 TV shows, including my favorite, *Rin Tin Tin*.

We did the pilot, and everybody acted as if it was a nothing show. *Daily Variety*'s review was tepid at best: "It's not only a small world as the title suggests for no reason at all," *Variety* commented. "But also small on provocation for putting it on film." Remington Rand, however, thought enough of the show to buy it. In those days, a sponsor picked up a show first and then took it to a major network. But they didn't like the name of the show. At first, Joe Connelly and Bob Mosher changed the name to *Wally and the Beaver*. Remington Rand said the title now sounded too much like an animal show. So Connelly and Mosher changed the title one more time to *Leave It to Beaver*.

Then they refined it. They wanted a character like Eddie Haskell, but they didn't think Harry Shearer from the pilot was right. They didn't feel Casey Adams was right for the father, so they replaced him with Hugh Beaumont. Paul Sullivan had grown too tall during the summer to play Wally and had to be replaced too. That's when Tony Dow came aboard. But no one ever questioned the selection of Barbara Billingsly as June Cleaver. "We never even interviewed another actress for the part," Joe Connelly said recently. "It was her part for the asking."

It's very difficult to find a person whom everyone unreservedly likes. But Barbara is just that person. Originally spotted by an MGM talent scout, she was signed to a long-term contract by the studio. She had lots of dramatic experience both on stage and screen before she entered the realm of TV in the early 1950s. Some of her motion picture credits include *The Guys Named Mike*, *The Bad and the Beautiful*, and *Half a Hero*. She toured on stage with Billie Burke, her dramatic mentor, and enjoyed musical comedy success with a featured role in *Roberta*.

A mother of two boys herself, Barbara combined the twin talents of motherhood and acting so effectively, that as my TV mom she has remained for many the true ideal of American motherhood. Barbara says:

> People often think I'm from New York because of my modeling career. But I was actually born in Los Angeles where I went to Washington High School with Esther Williams. I went to New York originally to do a play called *Straw Hats*. It was a whopping success. It lasted five days. Yet it was a good experience.
>
> So I decided to get a job modeling. Believe me, I didn't know what the heck I was doing. The man I worked for was Herbert Sondheim, composer Stephen Sondheim's father. They taught me how to walk across the room and all the basic modeling techniques. I had a fine old time. I stayed there for a while, got married,

went to Florida, had a child, and lived there for a while. Then we came back to California and had another child. They were the same ages as Wally and the Beaver, so I was at home with two children and on the set with two children.

I was fortunate enough to do a lot of television. I worked on the *Four Star Playhouse* with David Niven, Dick Powell, Ida Lupino, and Charles Boyer. I did *Schlitz Playhouse of Stars*. I worked on *Climax* with the great Ethel Barrymore. I was also under contract and did a picture with Clark Gable. I even have some stills of Clark Gable and me, which is a great thrill.

I did a series called *Professional Father* with Steve Dunne before I did *Leave It to Beaver*, which was live from CBS. I did about four *Matinee Theater* productions. They were good shows, with some of the finest writers in the business. So I had done a whole lot of varied work in my pre-June Cleaver days.

Fate dealt me a nasty blow in 1955, when my husband Roy Killino, a prominent film and television director, died suddenly, leaving me widowed at a rather young age. Enter Joe Connelly and Bob Mosher. I had originally met with Joe Connelly and Bob Mosher about doing another series with Buddy Ebsen. They were going to do a show with Buddy and they needed a wife. They were very kind, but it didn't happen because my husband had a heart attack and was gone.

Then six months later, Joe and Bob wanted to see me. I went to see them, and they just said that they wanted to see how I looked. They handed me a script, and said that they were going to do a pilot. That's how I got the part of June Cleaver. I don't think they looked at anybody else. The show was called *It's a Small World*.

It was a great script. The strangest thing about it is while Hugh and Tony weren't in it, the characters of Ward and Wally were. I knew it was a good show, but who could have guessed it would last all these years.

Jerry was just the cutest little boy. What impressed

me so much about him was that he wasn't acting. He was just being. We would go in Monday morning with a new script, and we'd all sit around the table. Jerry couldn't read, but my goodness, everything came out so naturally. He was absolutely perfect. He had something that was very special.

The show has held up, and I always give credit to Joe [Connelly] and Bob [Mosher]. I'm not taking anything away from the casting, but they wrote all the early shows. Even when they got some help later, they were right down on the set, watching and changing. They took everything from something that happened in their own children's lives. So the stories were based on fact. When Joe and Bob came on the set, they had one assistant. That was it. Today you have all these people sitting across the stage putting their two cents into things they know nothing about.

If Connelly and Mosher were determined to refine the show, the selection of Hugh Beaumont as Ward and Tony Dow as Wally was a stoke of sheer genius.

One of my real delights in the show was the casting of Hugh Beaumont as my TV father Ward Cleaver. Hugh was a very interesting man with quite a list of distinguished and varied credits in radio and movies. He played villains and tough guys. His films included *Objective Burma* with Erroll Flynnn, *Blue Dahlia* with Alan Ladd and Veronica Lake, *Phone Call from a Stranger* with Shelly Winters and Gary Merrill, and *Railroaded*, a taut *film noir* thriller directed by Anthony Mann. He was best known as RKO'S hard-drinking, tough-talking detective Michael Shayne.

Before *Leave It to Beaver*, one of the things I did was a religious show. A lot of people don't know it, but Hugh was a Methodist minister. He was posted to the clergy and was a conscientious objector during World War II. A triple-threat athlete in high school and college, he served as a medic in the war.

After the war, he transferred to the University of Southern California. He majored in religion and minored in social studies. While he was at theological school, he got married. He and his wife, Kathryn, then an aspiring actress, had a son, and soon he was posted to a very poor community as a pastor. The community was so poor, in fact, that it couldn't afford a full-time minister. To supplement his income he became a radio personality. He did lots of radio ads and radio shows, often playing the hard-drinking hard-smoking tough guys roles—kind of a Bogart on radio—which is about as far from being a minister as you can get. Even after he became a successful actor, he continued to work as a guest or interim pastor at many Los Angeles–area churches.

Hugh also maintained an interest in several other fields. As a writer, many of his stories appeared in magazines like the *Saturday Evening Post* and the *Ladies Home Journal*. In 1960, Hugh wrote an open letter to TV viewers thanking them for all the warm letters the show had received from parents across the country. He also directed some of our best *Leave It to Beaver* episodes, including a few of my personal favorites.

Now back to the religious show I mentioned. It was a Christmas Special, a high budget production at a major studio. Hugh Beaumont was playing a minister in an orphanage. Someone had stolen the children's toys, and I played one of the orphans whose toys were stolen. The scene required that I cry. Hugh Beaumont came up to me and asked, "Do you know how to cry?" And I said that I didn't know how. He seemed like a nice man, and I was always eager to take advice. He said, "You don't have to cry. All you have to do is cover your eyes and mouth and laugh. When people hear you laughing and you cover your eyes and mouth, they're going to think you are crying." He said laughter and crying are very similar. "Just try it and the director will say it's fine." And it worked!

When I saw Hugh interviewing for the part of Ward Cleaver, I had a real affection for him because I had worked with him before. I read with about eight or ten prospective fathers, but when I went home that night I prayed like crazy that Hugh Beaumont would get the part and he did.

Of course, Hugh and Barbara may well have been the most likable television parents of them all. Barbara always said that Hugh just became better looking the older he got, and that even after he got sick he was absolutely handsome with that shock of white hair. So I was a little taken aback when Barbara said that at first they didn't really get along that well. "He called me a Pollyanna, and that teed me off," Barbara revealed recently. "But we soon learned to get along very well, and we became great, great friends. I miss him dearly."

In the early 1970s, Hugh suffered a stroke that left his face partially paralyzed. Doctors told him he would never walk or talk again. But he did and later even did some directing with community theater groups. He died suddenly of a heart attack on May 16, 1982, while visiting his son in Munich. We all felt a tremendous loss. A short time later, when CBS aired *Still the Beaver*, his presence was with us throughout the entire filming.

Barbara and Hugh had both pursued professional acting careers. My acting career evolved from being a child model. But Tony Dow never gave a boyhood thought about acting. He was an outstanding young athlete who held some national records in swimming, and was the Junior Olympic diving champion. But there was an acting connection in Tony's family. His mother, Muriel Montrose, had been a former "Our Gang" actress, and a Mack Sennett Bathing Beauty who once understudied Clara Bow.

Unlike me, Tony remained in the industry after our *Leave It to Beaver* days, appearing in such television series as *Mr. Novak*, *Dr. Kildare*, *My Three Sons*, and *The Greatest Show on Earth*. Today, he is an accomplished director, and he has directed episodes of *Coach* and *Babylon Five*. A few years ago, he did a film called *It Came From Outer Space* for the Sci-Fi channel, as well as being involved in the producing end of the business. But let Tony take it from here:

> I was twelve years old and had absolutely no interest in acting: A friend of mine, named Bill Bryant, who was a lifeguard at the pool where I worked out, was also an actor. He was up for a series, and since we kind of looked alike he thought it might help him get the part of the father.
>
> So I put on my blue suit and went to Columbia Stu-

dios with him. They were doing a show called *Johnny Wildlife*, which was about a father and son living in the jungle. They needed a young boy who could jump off trees, dive into the water, and look athletic. I ended up with a part in the *Johnny Wildlife* series, but the series never sold.

It was fun. I enjoyed it. But I didn't think I was very good. My mom had an affinity for Hawaii, so we'd spend a couple of months there. I had picked up an agent for the *Johnny Wildlife* project, and he suggested that I should go on three more interviews. If nothing worked out, then off to Hawaii. My mother acquiesced. *Leave It to Beaver* happened to be one of the interviews.

It was really bizarre because the other two interviews also panned out and I got both jobs. One was for a Mouseketeer, and the other was for a boy in a Tarzan series. With the advice of the agent, my mom, and others in the know, we decided that *Leave It to Beaver* was the project to take on.

The guy who they had in the original pilot grew pretty quickly and became too tall for the part. They were looking for new people, and had seen everybody in Hollywood it seemed. Harry Ackerman, the executive producer of the show, worked on the pilot of *Johnny Wildlife*. He suggested that I should interview for *Leave It to Beaver*. I think hundreds interviewed initially. I feel I was lucky because they were under a time constraint.

Joe Connelly and Bob Mosher were smart guys. They understood that chemistry was important. They were very conscious that they wanted to have a cohesive unit.

I'm three years older than Jerry. I was struggling with the concept of being an actor, something that Jerry was very comfortable with. He was an old pro by then. In retrospect, he was amazing. He was one of those kids who never read a line wrong.

Norman Tokar, the main director in the early stages of the show, was just as important in making me an actor

as were Joe and Bob. They wrote the honesty. He made
it happen.

In the beginning I was floundering. I didn't know
what I was doing. Once I realized that I was an actor,
then I just tried to be as natural as possible.

The Cleaver clan was now complete. Once the show got off
the ground, others joined the cast as regulars: Frank Bank
(Lumpy), Sue Randall (Miss Landers), Stanley Fafara (Whitey),
and Steven Talbot (Gilbert). But no supporting cast member
would create as lasting an impression as Ken Osmond. As Wally
once said, "A character like Eddie Haskell comes along only once
in a hundred years."

TV Guide predicted that the 1957–1958 TV calendar would
be "a season to make your eyes pop." It promised fewer comedians, fewer quiz shows, and fewer hour-long dramas; and more
musical programs, more adult westerns, and more documentary
programs. *Gunsmoke* ruled the TV world with the highest ratings,
Howdy Doody was already celebrating its tenth birthday, and *The
Ed Sullivan Show, The Adventures of Ozzie and Harriet, Alfred Hitch-
ock Presents*, and *G. E. Theater*, starring Ronald Reagan, were
among the popular returning shows.

Viewers would miss *I Love Lucy*, the most popular series in
1956. With the unfolding of the 1957–1958 TV season, the experts
seemed to agree that one of the reasons comedy had taken a
nosedive was the constant straining for the belly laugh, or what
writer Hal Humphrey called "the big boff."

Humphry called attention to *Leave It to Beaver* in his September 30, 1957, column in the *Los Angeles Daily Mirror News: Amos
'n' Andy* Writers Try For New Laughs," he announced in plug-
ging the impending debut of the show. "Beaver is a 7-year-old
boy played by Jerry Mathers. He has a brother Wally (Tony
Dow), 12, and, of course, there is a mother and father (Barbara
Billingsly and Hugh Beaumont)."

The competition was heavy, and the fall season was vintage.
Also making their television debut that fall were *Perry Mason*,
with Raymond Burr, *Wagon Train* with Ward Bond and Robert
Horton, *Maverick* with James Garner and Jack Kelly, *Have Gun,*

Will Travel with Richard Boone as Paladin, *M Squad* with Lee Marvin, *Bachelor Father* with John Forsythe, and *The Real McCoys* with Walter Brennan. Was TV ready for a slow-paced comedy laced with charm, a series that showed the amusing and often contradictory world of adults through the eyes of two boys? A couple of guys named Connelly and Mosher were determined to give it a try. "We may die the death of a dog with this kind of show," Joe Connelly was quoted as saying, "but we are going to stick with the original premise. We're not going to hoke it up or strain for laughs."

chapter 7

Connelly and Mosher: The Best of the Best

Bob Mosher sat at his typewriter and I told stories. When something sounded good, he'd start typing. He was a brilliant writer and we made a hell of a team.
—*Joe Connelly, writer and creator of* Leave It to Beaver

All agree that Joe Connelly and Bob Mosher were extremely gifted and creative writers. Brian Levant, my good friend and creator of the *New Leave It to Beaver Show*, calls them the "Mark Twains of their day." Both were true professionals and very decent men.

Both were from New York State. Connelly was born in New York City and educated at the Roxburry School in Cheshire, Connecticut. Mosher was born in Auburn, New York, and educated at Susquehanna University in Pennsylvania. Together, the Mosher family and the Connelly family had nine kids between them. This gave them an insight into the ways and problems of kids that few writers could match.

The two first met as young writers in New York City, where they were employed by the J. Walter Thompson Agency. According to Rich Correll, his father Charles Correll, who with Freeman Gosden originated *Amos 'n' Andy*, first met Connelly in 1939 when he was a young man working at the New York World's Fair.

A number of years later, after Connelly and Mosher came to Hollywood, they submitted some work to Gosden and Correll, who liked their work immensely. Subsequently, Connelly and Mosher became the head writers of *Amos 'n' Andy* on radio. They translated the show to TV in 1950, where it was filmed at the Hal Roach Studios for CBS. They were already well-regarded radio writers who wrote shows for Edgar Bergan, Phil Harris, Frank Morgan, and many others before beginning their ten-year stint on *Amos 'n' Andy*.

After a failed venture with the *Ray Milland Anthology* series, they tried their hands with a movie script. Based on a situation at Connelly's son's parochial school, their script was eventually filmed as *The Private War of Major Benson*, starring Charlton Heston. It garnered an Oscar nomination for the writing team.

According to Richard Correll, who went to Loyola High School with one of Connelly's children, Ricky, Connelly told Charles Correll and the two boys that he wanted to write shows about his kids—he had seven children.

For the first couple of years Connelly and Mosher wrote all the shows. Then they became the executive producers and started hiring other writers. They were always having people submit scripts, and if they could use the scripts, they would refine them. After *Leave It to Beaver*, they wrote and created *The Munsters*.

Connelly had always wanted to be a writer. As a young man he kept a book recording his experiences. After he had children, he recorded their stories as well. If something happened at school and one of his kids said, "You know what happened to Joe Smith," Connelly would write it down. He also kept an index of names in the back of the book. If he met a "Jerry" or a "Herb," he wrote it down. During World War II, he served in the Merchant Marines. One of his shipmates was called the Beaver, and Connelly added it to his index of names.

When he and Mosher started formatting *Leave It to Beaver*, he began looking for a name for the little boy. He looked at his index and went through all the As, but nothing seemed to fit. He went through the Bs, and came to "Beaver," which he thought would make a good nickname for Theodore. And from

Beaver, came the name Cleaver. I wonder what happened to Mr. Connelly's shipmate Beaver; I'd like to tell him I've gone through life with his name.

Connelly and Mosher were as different as the proverbial night and day. Mosher was calm, deliberate, and quiet. His passions were playing the Hammond organ and collecting horseless carriages. Connelly was clearly the flamboyant type, a big two-fisted Irishman who was known to like a drink or two. During the terrible Bel Air, California, fire in the early 1960s, he broke through the police barricades, climbed to the top of his roof with fire hose in hand, and watered down his house and grounds. Then he fended off the evacuation teams with a .45 from his extensive gun collection. The result was that his was one of the few houses to survive the fire.

When the final episode of *Leave It to Beaver* was aired in 1963, Ward and June are looking through their picture albums. Employing flashbacks of earlier shows, they tell the boys that Wally had trouble saying the name of his little brother "Theodore." Somehow it came out sounding more like "Beaver." So the secret of how Theodore Cleaver became "the Beaver" was finally revealed at the end of the show's run.

In preparing the series, Connelly originally adopted a script based on his son Ricky: the things he liked to do, the movies he went to, the models he wanted to build, and the trouble he got into. When he sold the show, Ricky became the Beaver. Beaver Cleaver was really based on Ricky Connelly. The same holds true for the cast of friends. There was a blond kid, a tall kid, a short kid. Connelly made all that very clear. The real Larry Mondello, Terry Forte, got to be a very good friend of mine in real life. In a similar way, Richard Correll was working with me as the Beaver, and he also was friends with Ricky Connelly, whom his dad had patterned the Beaver after.

Most of the kids on the other big series would get no real vacation. Connelly and Mosher said this wasn't fair. The writers were always very concerned about us, and they felt we should have a real summer vacation. So they re-did the schedule. It cost them a lot of money because they had to shoot on shorter schedule at unusual times.

Interestingly, they didn't want Tony and me to watch the show on TV. They didn't want us to critique ourselves and do things differently. They always said, "Just be yourselves, be natural! We'll write the lines."

People ask me if I watched the show as a kid. I say, "No! I watched *Maverick*." The first year, *Maverick* was the main competition in our time slot. It was up for an Emmy for the best new show and so were we.

Connelly and Mosher used the same precision in choosing directors as they did in choosing writers. They landed some of the best. The directors they chose had to have the patience and skill to work with kids, and to pace the gentle humor of the scripts. Norman Tokar directed most of the episodes for the first three years. When asked why Connelly and Mosher counted so heavily on Norm Tokar, Connelly left no room for doubt. "Norman Tokar was the best in the business, and was well-suited for our show. We made good use of his great talents."

A former child actor who once played Henry Aldrich on the radio, Tokar also wrote many of the *Leave It to Beaver* shows. At the time he was directing the show, he was thirty-nine years old, with a warm pleasant smile and head of red hair. Tokar was primarily responsible for developing the characters of Eddie Haskell and Larry Mondello. Connelly and Mosher may have written Eddie Haskell into the show, but Tokar gave the impetus to the Eddie Haskell character. "I'm no Svengali," Tokar told *TV Guide* in a 1958 interview. "The thing about directing kids is the attention span. I mean the point beyond which boredom sets in. Keep them amused, interested and happy, and at the same time don't let them run roughshod over you."

And we had other outstanding directors as well. One of my favorites was David Butler. A longtime film director whose hit movies included *Road to Morocco, The Little Colonel*, and *Calamity Jane*, he also directed Shirley Temple. He would tell me stories about Bing Crosby and Bob Hope.

Norman Abbott directed most of the shows the last three years of the series. When he came back to direct some episodes of the *New Leave It to Beaver* in the mid-1980s, I saw him for the first time as an adult. I had missed so much because these guys were such great talents. They were pillars in their fields, yet as a kid I really knew them only as directors. They were the adult figures, and I just did what I was told. When Abbott directed the new show, we talked about his career and all the shows he had directed. A delightful raconteur, he told me wonderful stories about the industry and the people he had known.

These were great years for me. I went to all these different events like the Emmy Awards. I had a little tuxedo, and I sat there with a youthful bewilderment, and the joy of just being a kid in an interesting setting.

Leave It to Beaver's all-American town of Mayfield features landmarks aplenty: Grant Avenue Grammar School, Mayfield High, and the Hayden Memorial Library. Like towns everywhere, it even had a haunted house—the Old MacMahon House, later to become Herman Munster's house. We played ball at Metzger's Field, went boating at Miller's Pond, vacationed at Friends Lake, and bought gimmicks at Uncle Artie's Magic Shop. We could visit Captain Jack's Alligator Farm. (That's where Wally and the Beav bought the notorious Cleaver gator that put our first episode on hold.) Or we'd scrounge around Fats Flanagan's Junkyard in search of whatever. But where was Mayfield actually located? Well, let's just say that Mayfield is anywhere, USA. If you notice, there *are* some odd things about Mayfield. It's always spring or fall, and it never snows. It's usually sunny, unless the plot calls for rain. It's expensive to make rain, you have to set up rain machines and hire a special effects man.

Actually, there are twenty-seven Mayfields across the country. Sometimes people think it's Akron, Ohio, because there's a Mayfield near Akron. But at different times Mayfield is described as being only twenty miles from the ocean. Others think it is somewhere in California, but the characters travel to California. We even altered the mileage signs at the bus station when Beaver goes on a trip, so viewers wouldn't be able to go to their atlas and pinpoint the town.

We get requests from a few of the Mayfields to make appearances, thinking it will validate their town as the Mayfield of *Leave It to Beaver*. But the true location of Mayfield remains a mystery. That's why we've never taken one of the Mayfields under our wing. Connelly and Mosher knew exactly what they were doing.

Because the "Captain Jack" episode had been shelved by the CBS censors, we debuted on October 4, 1957, with "Beaver Gets 'Spelled." In Beaver lingo, 'spelled means getting kicked out of school. As all Beaver fans know, the kids from Mayfield had a vocabulary all their own: a "beaut" was a shiner in the eye, "heck" was the all-purpose curse word, and "messing around" was what the guys were doing when they weren't doing something they had to do. The show originally aired on Friday nights at 7:30 P.M. (EST) on CBS. Midway through the season, we were moved to Wednesday at 8:00 P.M. In the fall of 1958, we moved to ABC where we remained for the duration of the show.

Early in the series we did an episode called "Good Neighbors." Here was the first look at a character named Eddie Haskell, Wally's best friend. Obnoxious, mean, and a bully supreme, he is one of televisions best-loved and oft-quoted TV wise guys. He has aptly been described as the model white-collar delinquent. To Eddie, I was a "boy creep," a "shrimp," or a "squirt." His unctuous politeness to Ward and June is legendary. "Good Evening, Mrs. Cleaver. Mr. Cleaver." He was the guy everybody loved to hate.

I was amused to see, for example, that superstar Cher insists that it was not the Beaver or Wally, June or Ward, who made the greatest impression on her. The character on the show who impressed her most was Eddie Haskell "because I hated him so much. Later my son had this friend I never liked and I called him Eddie Haskell, because he reminded me of Eddie Haskell on *Leave It to Beaver*."

To evoke such visceral emotions in a sitcom requires a splendid actor. Of all of the fine performers associated with *Leave It to Beaver*, Kenny Osmond is the most talented of the lot. Unfortunately, he became so typecast as Eddie Haskell that his acting career hit the skids once the series closed.

All rumors that Ken was really chicken head–biting rock star Alice Cooper in disguise, or porn star John Holmes, are pure rubbish. In fact, Ken and his wife, Sandy, have been married thirty years and have two great kids. His oldest son, Eric, appeared as his son in the *New Leave It to Beaver Show,* and today works for Brian Levant. His youngest son, Christian, is doing post-graduate work in veterinary medicine.

Ken is also an actual hero. A Los Angeles police officer for seventeen years, he was shot four times in 1980 while in pursuit of a car thief. He was saved only by his body armor, his belt buckle, and his partner's courage. But let's turn the narrative over to Ken:

Unlike Jerry and Tony, my career was no accident. I had a typical movie mother. After school every day—even before I went to school—I went to classes: drama classes, dialect classes, ballet classes, ballroom classes, local theater, classes in everything you could ever imagine.

I was born in Glendale, California, and as a kid did all kinds of stage plays and a little theater. In 1949, I did my first film, *Plymouth Adventure.* I did at least one segment of every conceivable TV show that was on in the 1950s: The *Loretta Young Show, Lawman, Telephone Time, Mr. District Attorney, Ozzie and Harriet. Leave It to Beaver* was just another interview.

It was a cattle call. Every agent in town sent every kid they had. And through the process of elimination, I got lucky. Eddie was not intended to be a recurring role originally, as I understand it. But apparently the first show I did, called "New Neighbors," was so well liked that they brought me back a second time, then a third time. And it just worked itself in. In the original *It's a Small World,* there was an Eddie-type character who was probably the predecessor to Eddie Haskell.

Originally I read for Harry Ackerman. Then it ran up the chain of command. When I was selected, I didn't know anybody in the original cast. I think they had a basic idea of the type of character they wanted. The character of Eddie developed over the six-year period.

I think "New Neighbors" was the third show they shot. I was very fortunate in those early years of *Leave It to Beaver* to have worked with director Norman Tokar. He was outstanding, and helped me so much. A lot of people contributed to the character of Eddie Haskell, but I think Norman put the initial character there.

There weren't any funny lines in *Leave It to Beaver*. I think that one of the unique things about the show is that there are funny situations. But the lines were straight, which is totally different than the sitcoms today. Today it is set up, set up, set up, funny line. *Beaver* never had them.

People laugh because the situation Beaver was in, was a situation you were in as a child. People relate to it. I've heard it said that a kid like Eddie Haskell comes along only once in a lifetime. Nonsense! There is one in every neighborhood. There was one on your block when you grew up. His name was Tom, or his name was George. But he was Eddie.

There was a type of *Beaver* episode that I enjoyed more than the others. I still do today. Those were the episodes which show the raw underside of Eddie. Once in a while, not often, you could tell that Eddie was a human being. In his own special way, he would even apologize. You'd see that maybe there was a real person inside Eddie. I enjoyed that type of show.

During the original show, it was just kind of a way of life. Remember, I have no childhood memories of *not* being around the industry. So it wasn't good. It wasn't bad. It was just part of life.

If Eddie Haskell was the quintessential unctuous white-collar delinquent, Lumpy Rutherford was our version of the cowardly lion. "Oh, you needn't worry about Clarence," his mother once said. "When it comes to brains, he's got a head like the Rock of Gibraltar." In real life, brains are something that Frank Bank has plenty of. Frank went to UCLA, majored in finance, and for years has been a successful municipal bonds broker. He has handled the financial accounts of many of us associated with the show. Nor was Frank a cowardly bully like

Lumpy Rutherford. To the contrary, he wouldn't take any crap. Once while rehearsing *The Nanette Fabray Show*, a young actor with an irrascible reputation was giving Frank trouble and mouthing off to him. After trying to warn him to lay off, Frank hauled off and slugged the guy. The actor's name was Ryan O'Neal, soon to be the star of the hit movie *Love Story*.

On another occasion, we were getting ready to wrap up for the week. It was Friday afternoon, and they were shooting *The Ugly American* with Marlon Brando across from us, so we walked over to watch Brando and company. We were in our sixth season and were stars in our own right. Moreover, we were probably the least affected of all the kids on the various shows. Well, Brando looks at us and says, "Get these fucking kids off the set. Goddamn it, this is a closed set. I don't need these punk kids around there." Well, Frank just looked at him and said, "Eat shit, pal!" And we all turned around and walked away.

Sometimes it was very boring for Tony and me on the set. Since we were the only children who were regulars on the show, we spent a large part of our time alone. Every time we would make a noise somebody would yell, "Quiet on the set." To the crew we were not children, but professional actors. We had to be quiet all the time. Keeping two little, very bored boys quiet is not easy. I was really happy when Tony taught me how to play chess. It was the one game we could play where neither of us had to say a word or make any noise at all.

Frank Bank says:

I first appeared on the sixth show. There weren't that many fat kids around, so I was one of the onlys. I pretty much went in and read for the part. I don't know if it was originally supposed to be just a one shot deal, but it was very popular.

I was born in L.A., and acting was almost second nature for me. Yet I never really pursued it. I got in the movies strictly by accident. Back when I was a young kid, not all parents had cars. The fathers used to take the cars to work. But we were really rich, and my dad bought my mother a 1939 Willys for fifty bucks. So we were a two-car family.

This was 1949 and it was a real luxury. My next-door neighbor was in the movies. He was a kid named Whitey. One day, his mother asked if my mom could drive her and her son to the Ben Hecht studio. My mom said, "What am I going to do with Frankie?" She said, "Bring him along."

So we are sitting there and Whitey is inside talking to the casting director. A man walks in, takes one look at me and says, "You shouldn't be here today! Come back tomorrow!" My mother said, "Oh, my son is not an actor!" The man said, "He is now!"

She brought me back the next day and they cast me in a movie called *Cargo to Capetown* with Broderick Crawford and Mercedes McCambridge. I think it was Broderick Crawford's first film after he won the Oscar for *All the King's Men*. I got killed in the first five minutes. I got washed overboard in a ship.

I was in the *Will Rogers Story* with Will Rogers Jr. and Jane Wyman. My main claim to fame before *Beaver* was I was on radio as President of the Jack Benny Beverly Hills Beavers. When I went into the securities business, Jack was one of my clients before he died. All the jokes about him being cheap are the furthest thing from what he was. He was one of the most incredible men who ever lived.

I was Hollywood's fat kid. If there was a part in Hollywood for a fat kid it was me. It was like Jackie Coogan was the fat kid in the '30s and '40s, I was the fat kid in the '50s. I've been in 125 movies and TV shows. When the show was going, Jerry and Tony only did *Beaver*. Kenny and I did every show on the Universal lot. I was on *Bachelor Father, Cimmeron City, Wagon Train*, and the *Virginian*.

In 1961–1962—let's face it—the show helped build Universal in a big way. We were professionals. We didn't fool around. We used to spend a lot of time throwing a football or throwing a baseball around outside. We had a basketball hoop. As TV kids went, we were pretty normal. We can thank Hugh, Joe, and Bob for that. They were very big father figures, and they kept our asses straight.

In two distinct ways I was different from the rest of the kids. First of all I was the only Jewish kid in the group. I always kidded around and called myself the token Jew. But secondly, and this was important, I was the first to have my own car. I was older than the rest of the guys, so we'd all pile into my car and go downtown to Bob's Big Boy for lunch. When the big guys went out we'd always make Jerry sit in the backseat. "Mathers, you get in the backseat!" We always picked on the little kids and played practical jokes, and that's the way it was supposed to be. The first three years of the show, Jerry was cute. There were Larry Mondello and Judy Hensler. The second three years, Tony was a teenage idol. But Lumpy and Eddie were the assholes of the country. Jerry was a very good kid. He was friends with Richard Correll, Steven Talbot and the younger kids. Kenny, Tony, and I were friends. It was a division of power, just like in the show. It was an age thing, and the big kids usually won.

I think one of the best anecdotes I can give about Jerry happened when we were grown up. We were invited to an event in Santa Barbara. It was our show against a lot of other shows for a charity event. We were competing in athletic contests and having a good time knowing we were going to get money for charity.

Well, Jerry was one of our runners. I don't recall if he was our anchorman or not, but I'm telling you he was the fastest thing I ever saw in my life. Here's this "Irish Gnome," as I always called him, and he ran like the wind. It was either after the CBS Movie of the Week or the *New Leave It to Beaver* series. But I was shocked. I'm telling you he was as fast as grease lightning.

Our show was a family. Barbara Billingsly was America's mother—she is to this day. I think we were one of the most realistic shows on television, even though in the '70s they blasted us because June wore pearls, and Kenny and I were always getting Beaver and Wally in trouble. So be it! But Eddie and Lumpy were in everybody's life. We were there to be made examples of, and Ward was there to make examples of us every week.

The experience of *Leave It to Beaver* was the best! I think the public perceived us as being a pretty cool group. I loved being the good guy, although I was the bad guy of the good guys. It's always good to wear a white hat!

So here we are, June and Ward, Wally and the Beav, Eddie and Lumpy. We had become a TV family in the best sense of the term. Sooner or later, we would all go our separate ways, but never for very long. Our public would never allow it. There were always reunions and parades. Barbara and Tony would work together on the stage years later in *Come Blow Your Horn*. Then Tony and I would spend nearly two years doing dinner theater to packed houses across the country.

We would all be reunited again in 1983 for the CBS Movie of the Week, *Still the Beaver*; then for a second series called the *New Leave It to Beaver Show*, which did quite well on cable. Our 30th Anniversary in 1987 became a media event, laced with appearances and interviews across the country. The same for the 40th Anniversary. I found it even more gratifying than the original attention we got as children.

chapter 8

Being the Beav

My friends really liked Jerry. Of course, he was a big celebrity as kids go. He was always very humble about it. He didn't play it up big. He didn't want to draw attention to it.
—*Richard Correll*

Besides the quality of people involved with the show, there is another defining factor of *Beaver* that I can't emphasize too strongly. We were a show about child actors who grew up to be responsible adults. No drugs. No crime. No chronic complaints about being typecast forever. We became bankers, policemen, stockbrokers, and responsible family men. This is a cast that has never in forty years placed a blemish on the Cleaver family. Given current and past television history, that's fairly rare.

It helps explain the unique chemistry of our group. Yes, there have been times when things weren't as smooth as they might have been. We've had our concerns and disagreements over the years; our bridges haven't always crossed in perfect symmetry. But somehow we've always returned to home base. Today, after forty years, there remains a definite camaraderie.

I'm often asked how I was able to sustain the role of Beaver Cleaver, how much was really me? Did I get a scene and improvise my way through it? Is that the reason I always seemed so natural? Much of my screen presence was natural, I suppose. But one thing is certain, I did not improvise. My purpose was to do the very best job I could. Sure, actors will tell you that it's easier to say some lines than others. That's very true! Because I was dyslexic, I could think more in terms of concepts, so if I said a line in a particular way and it made sense, Connelly and Mosher would usually leave it in.

Our work routine was rigid, and our schedule demanding. Believe me it was work, and hard work! I would get up at 6:30 each morning, wash up, get dressed, and eat breakfast. Usually, my mother would drive me to the studio. It generally took about an hour to get there, and we began work at 8:00 sharp. Between shooting the scenes and going to school, we didn't leave the studio until 5:00 P.M. By the time I got home it was already 6:00 and dinnertime. During the winter months it was dark by 6:30, so this didn't leave much time for other things. My real fun time was the weekends.

Late Friday afternoon we received the script for the following week. We were to take it home and study it over the weekend. On Monday, we read the script at the studio, while Connelly and Mosher watched and listened, always taking notes and making intended revisions. On Tuesday, we'd rehearse all day. We'd go to the set and the director would start blocking shots. If we needed any unusual props, they made sure that all the props worked well. Then on Wednesday, Thursday, and Friday, we did the actual filming.

At about 10:00 or 11:00 each evening a driver would deliver script revisions to our homes. The revisions were in different colors depending on where we were with the script and the schedule. The original script was always white. Monday night revisions were pink partial pages. When we left the studio on Tuesday the final revisions had already been made. Then we'd go off book, meaning that we'd carry our scripts with us, but use them only when we really needed them. After Tuesday, if there was a need for revisions, these would be in yellow.

By Wednesday, the scripts were all set. The script girl came on the set, and if you missed a line she would call you on it, saying something like, "No, it's not written that way." Then we'd go back and do it the right way. Every so often a new script was needed, which could make things very hard on us. A script usually ran about 22 pages per episode.

Great credit goes to the writers. The scripts were so well written off the bat, that Tony and I fell easily into the pattern. But the concept of being brothers pretty much stopped when the shooting stopped. That's because we were segregated by age. He went to school with the older kids, like Ken Osmond and Frank Bank. I went to school with the younger kids, like Rusty Stevens and Steve Talbot. I was pals with the younger guys, and Tony was pals with the older actors. Because we went to different schools, we didn't really spend a great deal of time together during those early years.

This was no accident either. As parents themselves, Connelly and Mosher knew only too well that the little kids would try to emulate the older kids, and they'd be far better off keeping us apart. Tony and I would do a scene together, but when the scene was over, he'd go back to his school and I'd go back to mine. We wouldn't get together again until there was another scene to shoot.

Child actors in film or TV would work either from 8 A.M. to 5 P.M. or from 9 A.M. to 6 P.M. If they wanted to use us later than that, they had to have special permission from the Board of Education. If there was a night scene, we thought it was a big deal because they would let us come in at noon the next day. There were lots of restrictions.

Although all the adult actors on *Leave It to Beaver* liked the kids on the show, it was not true family-type affection. They were paid professional actors. We were paid professional actors. We all knew that our real family and friends were somewhere else waiting for us to come home. There lies the problem. "Never work with children or animals," W. C. Fields used to say. It is true. The relationship between the adult and child actors on the set can be strained. It is not a personal thing, but more of a professional reality. Children must, according to law, be off the set by 5 P.M., and they must go to school during the day. Adult actors must work around the children's schedule, even if that means that they sit on a set with nothing to do for hours and then work until midnight. The adults had to be back at the studio at the same time the following morning, regardless of the hours they had worked the previous night. Hugh Beaumont, Barbara Billingsley, Richard Deacon, and others were our coworkers and were nice to us based on that professional relationship. They never complained to us about having to work around us for seven years, but now looking back, I realize how frustrating it must have been for them. When we were home tucked in our beds, they were still filming, drinking coffee to stay awake.

Hugh Beaumont would play basketball with us once in a while. Hugh suffered a terrible trauma after we shot the pilot of the show, and it affected his mood for the run of our series. Every year Hugh and his family would drive from their home in Minnesota to California. Due to the filming schedule of our first episode, Hugh flew to Los Angeles, and his son drove the family car to Los Angeles. During the drive the car went off the road in Texas. The accident killed Hugh's mother and seriously injured Hugh's wife and son.

In Hugh's mind, I think he felt that if not for *Leave It to Beaver* he would have been driving that car and his mother would not have died. I don't know for sure, but I think it took the fun out of his success on the show. It became just a paying job.

Most of the television shows today are filmed inside a sound stage with three cameras and videotape. It is much less expensive to film a show this way. The entire crew is not needed until Friday, the filming day. Only one or two sets are used. There is no outside shooting. The actors have four days to rehearse until filming. It is much easier to put the show together and edit. Modern technology!

Leave It to Beaver was shot on 35mm film, like a movie. We used one camera, and much of the show was filmed outside. It took four days to shoot. The full crew had to be there every day we worked. The show was edited like a movie. In its day, the $45,000 per week *Leave It to Beaver* production cost was considered expensive. In comparison, the one-camera 1989 version of *New Leave It to Beaver* cost $800,000 per week to shoot.

When we weren't shooting scenes or going to class, I was basically having lots of fun every day. Remember there were seventy or eighty people who had a vested interest in keeping me happy. There was so much to see and do around the studios. For example, we'd go running in the back lot and see actor John Payne doing Westerns. I was very interested in guns and later became a collector myself, so I was just thrilled when he showed me the six shooter he was using. I particularly remember the day Ann-Margret brought her mother to the set. She was only seventeen or eighteen and was making *Bye Bye Birdie*. She wanted to show her mother the *Leave It to Beaver* set. I think I became aware of my impending puberty that day.

When I was making *That Certain Feeling* with Bob Hope at Paramount, Spencer Tracy and Robert Wagner were making *The Mountain* right across from us. I strolled onto their set and watched with amazement as they brought in all the snow to surround an airplane that had crashed. The stage was littered with actors who were supposed to be dead bodies.

Another film that stands out is *Prince Valiant*, again starring Robert Wagner, and with James Mason and Janet Leigh. I'd see these guys on the back lot dressed to the hilt and practicing with big broad swords. I'd go to the commissary to see them eating their lunch in full costume. What fun! But I was always aware that this was just make-believe. Just like me, these actors had a script and lines to say.

During *Leave It to Beaver*, the studios set up a basketball court for us. During lunch hour all the guys on the set would play a game of basketball. Between scenes we'd often play baseball and football. One day we were playing baseball and Tony Dow swung at a pitch. He got good wood on the ball and slugged it, breaking the window of Steve McQueen's car as he was driving by.

We were really scared. In those days, the cars were so loud that the studio put blinking red lights outside the stages when filming was in progress. When actual film was being shot, you had to stop your car. When McQueen was driving by the red light was on because someone else was filming a scene on our set. When he stopped, Tony's ball hit the driver's side of the window and shattered the glass. But Steve was very nice about it.

When Lee Marvin was doing *M Squad*, he came over and

tossed the football around with us. Marvin was a great athlete and a very tough man—he had been a combat Ranger during World War II. For someone so active, being in a movie studio all day could get boring. So when he wasn't shooting, he would make it a point to come over and throw the ball around with us.

At Universal we used to see Jack Webb a lot. Our chief fascination was that *Dragnet* was done completely on TelePrompTers. This machine ran typewritten words across a screen so you could read directly from it if you forgot a line. When we would do charity ads or commercials, they would take us to Jack Webb's set to use the TelePrompTers. It was the only set on the Universal lot that had the machines. There was a special guard at the door, and no one was allowed to enter, which of course added to the intrigue.

As at Paramount Studio, one of my favorite places at Universal was the commissary. Boy was it busy, and just about anyone might me there. You didn't have an inkling who you might run into. Try to imagine being a kid and seeing people in Roman soldier gear as they were filming *Spartacus*. On a given day you could walk into the commissary and see knights in full armor, spacemen in shiny attire, and a posse of rugged cowboys eating their lunch.

The commissary at Universal had a hierarchy of sorts. There were three distinct places to eat. People who needed a quick sandwich would grab a meal at the counter. The second eating tier was a restaurant with tables. If two or three people wanted to get together here for a meal, it featured good food and decent service. In the back of the commissary was an elegant restaurant called the Sun Room. Here the tables were covered with cloth and the waiters wore white vests. It was mainly for executives, big stars, and VIPs.

One of my biggest thrills was seeing my hero Audie Murphy in the commissary. I liked to play war, and as most people know, before he became a movie star, Audie Murphy was the most decorated American soldier of World War II. Barbara Stanwyck was very interesting because she sometimes ate at the counter. Many people couldn't understand why such a big star—an

Academy Award–winning actress—would eat at the counter. But she usually was in a hurry and didn't seem to mind what people thought.

Eating in the Sun Room required a reservation. It meant much better service, and a much bigger tip was expected because it was so elegant. Because of this, we rarely ate there. The regular restaurant was just fine for my mother and me. Anyhow they learned what I liked to eat and always had it ready for me. One of the things they put on the menu especially for me was a peanut butter and jelly sandwich. I just loved that as a kid. As I got a little older I started eating chili, which gave the wardrobe people fits. Because of course I would inadvertently spill chili on my shirt. Because we always had five of the same item of clothing, the wardrobe people would have to send back all five shirts. It was necessary for each identical shirt to look exactly the same when under the sensitivity of the camera's lens.

My favorite Sun Room story involves my good pal Richard Correll. Richard was an unbelievable monster fan. He was such a monster buff in fact, that Connelly and Mosher decided if he was so interested in monsters, then maybe other kids were too. This is how they got the idea for the *Munster* series.

Richard started acting professionally as an eight-year-old on *Love that Bob*, a mid-1950s sitcom with Robert Cummings. It worked well for him and he soon landed an agent. He did a number of television shows, then his father suggested to Joe Connelly that Richard come to Universal.

I first worked with Richard Correll on *Leave It to Beaver* in an episode called "The Spot Remover." We practically had the whole show together and spent the week talking about models and monster movies. He invited me to his home in Holmby Hills, a very fashionable section of Los Angeles between Beverly Hills and Bel Air. We found out we were just as compatible off the camera as on the camera, and we started to have a real good time together. I invited him home to Canoga Park and we spent the day playing games and talking. He always enjoyed a stay at my house. He was particularly fond of my dad, because while my dad was a stern disciplinarian, he knew how to get along with kids and made Richard laugh. Later he'd spend weekends with us and had so much fun with us that he didn't want to go home.

When I first met Richard, *Monster Magazine* was already on the market. In fact today Richard has a wall in his den with all sorts of original monster heads, which are collector's items, including *The Creature from the Black Lagoon*.

So now I've set the scene for the Sun Room story. As I mentioned, the Sun Room was located at the very back of the commissary. The huge windows were draped with plants outside so you couldn't look in. I was eating in the Sun Room (I think I had an interview), and so was Boris Karloff, who was filming his show, *Boris Karloff Presents*. Now Richard and Rusty Stevens (Larry Mondello) were huge fans of Boris Karloff. All of a sudden, crawling through the jungle-like brush were Richard and Rusty, and they are pressing their faces against the glass. The big problem is that it's a one-way glass. So they are trying like hell to see in and they couldn't, but everybody in the Sun Room could see their faces pressed against the glass. "Who are these crazy kids, and what are they trying to do," people wanted to know. Well, Richard and Rusty didn't get to see the great Karloff that day, but I'll never forget my two bewildered pals so comically trying to look through a one-way window in pursuit of a hero.

I'd walk around the studio and see bisons and cows. There were always a few horses readily available from whatever Western they might be shooting at the time. If they were doing *Wagon Train* with Ward Bond and Robert Horton, for example, the horses were in front of the stage. By stage I actually mean huge warehouses—perhaps 30,000 square feet. If horses were needed for a background scene, at a moment's notice wranglers would grab the number they needed and lead them on the stage. As soon as they were finished, they'd lead them back off so they wouldn't make any noise.

Universal was just remarkable. It was more than a city; it was a huge company laden with whatever directors and writers they might need to make their imaginary places come to life. One day you might have those extras charging over the hill for *Spartacus*. It looked like Rome but it was the back hills of Universal. The very next day you had Audie Murphy attacking Nazis on that same hill.

Each main actor on *Leave It to Beaver* had a dressing room on wheels where they could change clothes, with a couch and a little desk. But we also had a far nicer permanent dressing room where we could relax and keep our personal things. I had my own baseball glove, but it wasn't the glove I used on the show. The mitt I used on the show belonged to the prop man and wasn't a good baseball glove at all, certainly not one I would have wanted for myself back then. The same went for my lunch box on the show. Like the baseball mitt, it belonged to the prop man. He had this big prop box and would hand me the lunch box before the show, and I would give it back to him when we finished shooting.

But my green baseball cap is another story. It really belonged to me. On the first day at Revue, I had worn that great baseball cap. Our director Norman Tokar took one look and said, "What a great-looking cap. Leave the baseball cap on for the little boy." This just astounded our wardrobe man, Hughie McFarland, a real nice fellow. Remember, wardrobe had five or six pair of backups for each piece of wardrobe. The cap was my own, but McFarland figured he could find more hats that looked just like it. Well, they started shooting the first episode, and after seeing the rushes the next day Connelly and Mosher said, "That cap looks just great. Whenever he's outdoors we want him to wear that baseball cap."

Hughie McFarland tried and tried for years, but he could never find a baseball cap that matched it. They actually brought in a haberdasher and worked for weeks trying to copy that hat, but for some reason they could never get the same look. So I still have that green baseball cap from my *Leave It to Beaver* days. It's the *only* one I ever wore, and I will probably donate it to the Smithsonian one day.

My very favorite place on the Universal lot was the makeup lab. I would go there between takes when they were filming other parts. If Tony was shooting with someone else or if I had an hour or two of free time after finishing school, I'd spend it at the makeup lab.

It took about three minutes to walk there. Above the makeup department was a huge room where they had all these marvelous different masks lining the walls. They had Bela Lugosi and Boris Karloff death masks. There was Frankenstein and the Wolfman. The whole works. The makeup men would make a plaster mask. Then they would build the makeup for you, placing latex over your face so they could sculpt it to perfection. When they were doing *Spartacus*, Woody Strode was crucified upside down. They had to make an entire body cast out of latex so they could hang him upside down on the cross without hurting him.

The makeup men were always very nice to me. They would let me make scars and mustaches for myself and they would allow me to mix different things to make blood. We had two makeup men who I liked very much: Lester Burns and Bob Dawn. Dawn's father Jack did the makeup for *The Wizard of Oz*, and was reputed to have been the best in the business. Both Burns and Dawn were superb at their craft. In fact, after *Leave It to Beaver*, Dawn became famous for making all the masks for *Mission Impossible*.

I had a personal hand in making a mask that perhaps is one of the most famous in movie history. Dawn got a skull from a medical surplus house and let me help him with his project. A new skull is bright white because it's been bleached. We had to age the skull by putting yellow and brown lines on it, then rubbing them off. Because the mask was Anthony Perkins' mother in *Psycho*, we had to put hair on it.

Every day we'd comb all the hairs through. You had to place it piece by piece, dipping it into the glue and gluing it to the head. This went on for three or four weeks. Every chance I got I would run to the makeup lab and help Dawn glue the hair on the skull for *Psycho*. It's actually the one they used in the film.

People often can't believe that the Cleavers' house was not a real house at all. It was just flats and walls that could be moved. There's the appearance of a real house out there, but it doesn't have any innards. Because our TV home was really just sections of flats and walls, they were always bracing the walls by tearing things down. This leads to my boat story.

I found a flat one-by-two-foot piece of wood. I decided to

build a boat with it, so the first thing I did was ask one of the grips to cut it. The next thing was to find a piece of dowel for the sail. Well, Dawn and the prop man looked at it and said, "Oh, let us help you!" They started by weaving about eight or nine pieces of wood together. To give it depth, they glued it. They offered to send it to the woodshop and have it cut out in the shape of a boat. But since it was a small boat it would need a keel. So they sent it over to the special effects department, where they mounted a piece of lead on the bottom. Then they decided they needed a sail, so they sent it to the wardrobe department, where they made two sails for it. Then it went back to special effects, where they decided that because it was wood it should be fiberglassed. Then Dawn carved a skull in the front and painted it black. So, what started as a little project for me, was suddenly this huge studio production of building me a boat. It ended up costing the studio about $3,000 because all the departments had to bill them. So it's probably the most expensive sailboat of its size that you'll ever see.

The end result was a sailboat only twelve to sixteen inches long that wouldn't float. We tried, but the lead weight was so deep that as soon as you put it in the water it would flip over. But it's a very nice fiberglass boat and it makes a nice standup on the mantel. I still have the "Black Raider" today. But I would have been just as happy had they taken that one little piece of pine, drilled a hole in it, and made a boat that I could have just sailed around the lake.

Even before *Leave It to Beaver*, when I was doing movies, we'd go to different studios and there would be all sorts of food to eat, like doughnuts and cereal in the morning. People would lay out my clothes for me. I received bundles of favors and gifts, even truckloads of gifts at Christmastime. Everybody fell over backwards catering to me. In other words, I was spoiled rotten. But I didn't forget the sheer reality that I was a kid actor who was earning a living at my craft. I may have been spoiled rotten as the Beaver, but sanity quickly prevailed once I arrived home and my parents would say, "Go to your room! Pick up your clothes! Don't be late for dinner!" In the studio, I could take off my clothes and throw them on the couch. People would run in and pick up after me. Makeup people made sure my hair was combed just right. But then I went home, and boy were things different. It was back to normalcy.

chapter 9

Me and
the Beav:
The Universal
Connection

This show is no Henry Aldrich. The kids will not talk in radio type jokes, nor will there be any big laughs from the kids.

—*Bob Mosher to Hal Humphrey,*
  Los Angeles Mirror News,
  September 30, 1957

In the beginning, the show went largely unheralded mainly because CBS was pouring the bulk of its publicity money into what it considered the bigger guns. Yet as the year went on, *Leave It to Beaver* quietly pushed up the Neilsen ladder. *TV Guide* called me "Tom Sawyer, Junior Grade," and the Beaver "television's portrait of a typical American boy."

The critics were taking another look. John Crosby, one of our earliest boosters in the media, wrote that "the plots of the *Beaver* show are the sort of things that anyone's kids might get into, and the dialogue has that wonderful candor and directness." Wally, he explained, was "teetering precariously on the edge of adolescence," while the Beaver keeps yanking him back into the "trusting innocence of childhood." *TV Guide* added that "most of the delight stems from Beaver's wholly natural small-boy approach of life." The fact is, Connelly and Mosher repeatedly told our parents not to talk about the show when we were around because "the minute they turn into kid actors the show is dead."

Lots of people seem to think that CBS dropped us at the end of the first year. Nothing could be further from the truth. Back then, it was the sponsor who sold a show to the network, and Ralston Purina, our new sponsor, saw brighter times ahead with ABC.

Another factor that should be cleared up is Beaver's special way of talking. This was not the way I talked, nor did I invent this speech pattern for the show. Rather, the language was largely written in by Connelly, who borrowed it from his own son Ricky. It was really only a matter of dropping the first syllable of a word. According to Connelly, one night he asked one of his sons where his books were. His son replied, "I most got 'em." He asked his son the same question again, and received the same abbreviated answer. He asked his wife what the boy was saying. She didn't know either. Finally, his son looked up at his dad and patiently said, "I almost forgot them." Connelly said, "Oh!" And Beaver Cleaver was born.

As Wally and the Beaver, Tony and I played off one another very naturally. Of course, we had the benefit of excellent scripts and superb directors. But there was one time when things didn't exactly work out well for me and provided the most embarrassing moment I ever had on TV.

It had nothing to do with one of the episodes per se. Rather, it was a nationally syndicated show called *Commander Cody*. Space programs were very popular in the late 1950s, and the actor who played Commander Cody would show old *Flash Gordon* films and other films with space-related themes. He invited Tony and me to his show as Wally and the Beaver.

Commander Cody was talking to the kids, and the gag was that Tony and I were very excited about going on the spaceship. The Commander is talking and the kids are looking directly into the camera with great anticipation. The big ploy was that he started each episode by saying to the kids, "Put on your magic glasses!" So, Commander Cody finishes his interview with Wally and the Beaver, and then says, "OK, now we're going to watch Flash Gordon. OK, kids. Now put on your crash helmet and your magic glasses. Come on, Wally! Come on, Beaver! Let's watch *Flash Gordon*."

Before the show, we were taught to place our little fingers on either side of our chins. Then, with our palms up, we were to turn our hands back, making a circle with each hand by putting the thumb and first finger together. When we put the circles together in front of our eyes, it looks like glasses.

Tony goes zap, zap, and up went his magic glasses. No problem. But I'm having trouble. "Come on, Beaver, put on your magic glasses," the Commander repeats. "It's simple!" I try and try but I still can't seem to do it. Here I am on national television trying to put on my magic glasses, and nothing seems to work.

Well, I never got my magic glasses on! I never even came close. For two minutes Commander Cody bent and twisted my arm. "Come on, Beaver! You can do it! Put on those glasses! Come on, Beaver! Push! Push!" Then Tony tried. The two of them almost broke my arm. Still nothing worked. It was live TV and everybody was very embarrassed. Finally, Commander Cody gave up. "Well, Beaver just won't watch," he says. "We'll tell him about it!"

When it came to girls, Beaver wasn't exactly a patient sort. "Go see a girl? I'd rather smell a skunk!" This was the Beav's professed attitude. "If I had my choice between a three pound bass and a girl, I'd take a three pound bass." In Mayfield USA, red-blooded little boys were supposed to hate girls. They're not like the guys—you can't wrestle with them, they don't like blood or dirt. They're not even sugar and spice. They're just plain trouble. "Girls are rats," he tells Wally, "they're even rats in Sunday school." Beaver tells June that even if he gets married, he isn't going take his wife anywhere, not even Disneyland. June asks Beaver why he would say a thing like that. Beaver replies that "just 'cause you're married, that doesn't mean you gotta like girls."

Of course, Wally is turning fourteen and beginning to have different views on the feminine equation. The fact that blond-haired, blue-eyed Tony Dow was being compared to a youthful Robert Stack, only lent credibility to Wally's heartthrob status at Mayfield High. The battle of the boys and girls remained a recurrent theme in the show. I should also point out that the show proved every bit as popular with women and girls as it did with boys and men. The July 1959 issue of *TV Star Parade* ran a feature on Tony and me entitled "Who Needs Girls? The Beaver and TV Brother Enjoy Carefree Bachelor Life." But this didn't minimize the fact that I would get a hundred proposals of marriage a week from girls under ten.

But really, there weren't many girls around, as surprising as it may seem. The only girls that I would see were those I worked with. And because we weren't allowed to talk on the set, I didn't get to know them very well.

Of course, Veronica Cartwright as Violet Rutherford gave me my first TV kiss. But the sad truth is that I don't even remember the first girl I ever actually kissed. I know that's terrible. In high school I had girlfriends and I kissed them, sure! But I don't remember the first one. So that first kiss that most kids recall must not have been too wonderful for me. I went to an all-boys high school, but until my junior year I never dated on my own. Basically we'd go to sock hops, dance in the gym, and then go home.

But *Leave It to Beaver* did give me my first taste of true love, even if mostly it was limited to the category of pure fantasy. Her name was Beverly, and she was one of the secretary's daughters. I'd see her only when we did the show. She was an extra on the show, and once when I was having a pool party, she and her mother Kitty came by. Richard Correll and a couple of the kids came over, and we made hamburgers and swam in the pool most of the day. That was it!

The most embarrassing thing that ever happened with Beverly was something the Beaver himself could have gotten into. Once during the shooting of an episode, we had a substitute teacher, who tried to show me little tricks, thinking I might like him better.

It was between shots and all the kids in the class, including Beverly, were there. The idea was to send me out of the room and ask any of the kids to say a word. And then when they named the word I would come in and he'd say, "Jerry, I want you to think of a word." The trick was that he would tap on the board. When he tapped three times that meant I had the first letter of the word. Then he'd ask me another question, and another question, and every time I would get the right signal.

The first word was something like clown. I got it and the kids said, "Oh, he has mental telepathy." They sent me out of the room again, this time Beverly picks the word "shirt."

Well I went up to the board and I listened to all the dots and dashes and I wrote it on the board. The first letter was "s," and I wrote it down. The next letter was "h," and I wrote it down. The same for the third letter "i." Boy, am I on a roll. So I now have s h i _ _. But somehow I don't connect with the fourth letter "r." But I did pick up on the fifth letter. I didn't want to write the whole word until I was sure I had it. Now I thought I did, and I felt very proud. I had out-foxed the pack. When the teacher asked me if I had it, I said, "Yes," and wrote SHIT, and everyone just cracked up. I looked at it and was real embarrassed. My friend Richard Correll looked at it, shook his head and said, "Don't you know what that means? How could you write that?" I looked at Richard, just like the Beaver might have looked at Wally, and said, "That's what the guy told me, Richie. I missed the 'r' in shit."

And of course I was getting all this attention, and I was rolling along with a steady flow of adulation. *TV Guide* labeled Tony and me (ages 12 and 9) among the "eight top young freshmen on the television campus" for the Class of 1957. The others included Jon Provost (age 7) as the replacement for Tommy Rettig (16) on *Lassie*, Angela Cartwright (5), as the youngest of the three offspring on *The Danny Thomas Show*, Gale Stone (12) and Karen Green (13) on *The Eve Arden Show*, Mike Winkleman (11) on *The Real McCoys*, Bobby Clark on *Casey Jones*, and Noreen Corcoran in *Bachelor Father*.

When I worked at the studio, at Christmastime a truck would come by filled with nothing but presents. Every prop man, the forty or fifty people working on the set, all the executives, and all the secretaries felt obligated to buy me a Christmas present.

Everyone from studio heads down would send presents. They tried to outdo each other. Susie would get presents too, but she would be a bit aggravated because most of the presents were boys' toys. The heads of the studios would give the most elaborate gifts. The directors always gave good gifts too. If said in an interview that I collected rocks as a hobby, you can bet that at Christmastime thousands of rocks were sent to me. The same thing with World War II antiques and other military collectibles.

Each year, the studio sent us several big boxes of See's candy. Susie and I would poke the bottom of the box to see what candies we liked best, so they were all pretty much ruined by the time we were through with them. The studio also wanted me to do publicity every weekend, but my parents wouldn't allow it. Six times a year was the limit they set.

I must credit my family again in explaining how I managed to keep my childhood in proper perspective. Perhaps this is best illustrated in an interview with my father that appeared in Hal Humphrey's column in the *Los Angeles Mirror News* on February 28, 1959. Humphrey, the TV-Radio editor for the *Mirror News* captioned his column "How Would You Treat a Little 'Beaver'?"

What would you do if you were harboring a ten-year-old actor in your home who's income was as much or more than your own?

Norman Mathers, ex-Air Force Pilot and schoolteacher finds himself in this spot. He's the father of little Jerry Mathers, the Beaver in ABC's successful *Leave It to Beaver* series.

"If Jerry's being in this TV series becomes too much a problem for him or the rest of us, he will be out of it the next day," states Norman firmly.

Should Jerry himself become bored or unhappy with his lot as a TV star, his father has the right to cancel the contract with Gomalco Productions, the George Gobel-Dave O'Malley Company which finances *Leave It to Beaver*.

It isn't likely that Norman Mathers will ever take such a drastic step any more than it is likely that young Jerry will become a two-headed ham dracula.

Norman and Marilyn Mathers are fully aware of the

pitfalls confronting both Jerry and themselves. There are plenty of precedents illustrating the conniving "stage parents" and the precocious brat of an offspring.

"We make a conscious effort to see that Jerry lives a normal life with his brother and sister and other kids in the neighborhood," says Norman. "When he gets into trouble of his own making, he is spanked."

My father quite typically thanked Hal Humphrey in a letter dated March 3, 1959, on Birmingham High School stationery. At the time my dad was a counselor at the school.

Mr. Hal Humphrey
TV and Radio Editor
Los Angeles Daily News

Dear Hal:
I want to thank you on behalf of myself and the *Leave It to Beaver* show for your fine article. I was delighted with the way it turned out.
Keep up your excellent work as TV Editor and I hope that before long we might get together for lunch again.
Thank you again.

Sincerely,
Norm Mathers

Hal Humprey's point is well taken. I made a good amount of money as a child actor, and my money did help to support my family. So what! How many children who made money in other ways turned their paychecks over to their mother and father to help them pay the mortgage, purchase food, or support other family members? I only did what was right. I am proud that my money helped my parents buy a nice house for our family. Maybe I made the money, but my brothers and sister had to do without a full-time mother when she was at the studio with me. Maybe my sister Susie would have been a child star too, if my mom had had the time to take her on interviews. My family gave me love and emotional support then and now. Whatever financial support I gave them was well worth the trade. My father had a good job. My mother's job was to see that I did a good job. If I was out of work, the family would and could survive. By contrast, many child stars supported their parents. If the kids were out of work, so were the parents.

My mom and dad gave me a fine home. They loved me. They drove me to interviews and provided a normal life for me. Ward Cleaver, my TV dad, might have taken Beaver into the den to counsel him and said, "Son, the family is a team and we all support each other. If each member of the family thinks only of himself, then the whole team loses." This was my philosophy then, and it's my philosophy now! Like all families, we fought from time to time, but an attack on one of us from the outside was an attack on all of us. To this day we are a solid family unit.

By 1960, another Mathers joined the ranks of show business when my younger brother Jimmy joined the Screen Actor's Guild. Jimmy is seven years younger than I am, and for better or worse ended up looking a whole lot like me. Interestingly, someone once sent me a picture with a caption that read, "Jerry Mathers and Elizabeth Montgomery." The picture was from an episode of *Bewitched*, and the person wanted me to autograph it. I would have been glad to, except the little Mathers boy in the photo was not me, it was my brother Jimmy. That's how much we looked alike.

Perhaps because my name is so well known, a lot of people don't realize what a talented fellow my brother Jim really is. He had co-starring roles in films like *Summer Magic* with Haley Mills and Burl Ives, *Mail Order Bride* with Buddy Ebson and Keir Dulea, and *The New Interns* with George Segal. Then Connelly and Mosher cast him as Benji Major in a new series called *Ichabod and Me*. Jimmy continued acting well into the 1970s, appearing in such shows as *Bewitched*, *My Three Sons*, *The Munsters*, and *Adam-12*.

A proud moment for both of us came when *TV Guide* featured a photograph and a blurb of the Brothers Mathers in a piece called "Oh, Brother: In Hollywood, Success is Sometimes a Family Affair." The other brother teams included Rex and Rhodes Reason, Johnny and Bobby Crawford, and Dwayne and Darryl Hickman.

Jim has remained in the business for thirty years. He began working behind the camera in 1975, and has been director of photography on more than twenty feature films and innumerable television series and TV specials. Being seven years younger, Jimmy grew up knowing me as a television star. When my two youngest brothers Shaun and Patrick were born, I had already left show business and was attending Notre Dame High School.

Meanwhile the show was receiving increasingly favorable reviews. As we approached our first season on ABC, *Time* magazine called *Leave It to Beaver* "The most appealing of family comedies since Henry Aldrich." *Variety* said it was "consistently a sound show" and Harriet Van Horn in the *New York World Telegraph-Sun* said, "I've lost my heart to Jerry Mathers."

John Crosby in the New York *Herald Tribune* still called our show "one of the funniest." Larry Walters in the *Chicago Tribune* was particularly flattering, commenting that "What Tom Sawyer and Huck Finn, and Penrod and his pals, were to my generation, Beaver and Wally are to the youngsters of today."

Look magazine called us "the most applauded situation comedy of the season. . . . *Leave It to Beaver* evokes a humorous and pleasurable nostalgic glow." But I'd like to think that Willaim Ewald of the *United Press* was most on target when he said, "In situation comedies. . . . *Leave It to Beaver* is the class of its field."

At Revue, Gamalco Productions, formed by comedian George Gobel and baseball mogul Dave O'Malley, produced our shows. Gobel it seems was looking for a good investment for some leftover money. During our third season in 1959, *Leave It to Beaver* moved from Revue on the Republic Studio lot to Universal Studios. The move to Universal was auspicious to say the least. It was the start of an association between the studio and the *Leave It to Beaver* crowd that has continued to the present day.

When TV intruded on the motion picture scene in the 1950s, there was a real need for change. Universal was floundering and was acquired by MCA (Music Corporation of America), an organization of ex-agents and TV producers in 1959, and became known as MCA/Universal. Before that, MCA had run the television department at Revue. So when MCA bought Universal they took their entire stock of TV shows with them.

The studio was now presided over by one of the most brilliant entertainment moguls in Hollywood history—Lew Wasserman—who first formed MCA into one of the most successful talent agencies on the world entertainment scene. Together with Paul Donnelly, the studio's vice president of Television and Motion Pictures, and Donnelly's young legal intern Sid Sheinberg, MCA/Universal was transformed into one of the best known TV and motion picture studios.

Leave It to Beaver was one of MCA/Universal's first shows, and we became part of the MCA family. Mr. Wasserman always treated us beautifully. He would visit the set regularly to see "his boys," offering us sage advice on the value of college and the avoidance of most vices.

Leave It to Beaver remains one of the most successful syndicated television shows in the Universal vault. It makes money not only in reruns throughout the world, but in the sale of film clips and merchandising. When an advertising campaign needs to show a symbol of the 1950s in a commercial, they might purchase a clip or picture from the show. Hallmark Greeting Cards has a *Leave It to Beaver* collection in their Shoebox Division. In forty-one years the money has not stopped flowing into the Universal vault and Universal has marketed the young faces of Tony Dow, Ken Osmond, and myself very well.

My parents had been very insightful regarding merchandising rights of my likeness. In 1957 they asked for and received 10 percent of all gross income made from merchandising my face as "The Beaver." In 1984 an MCA/Universal Studio executive decided that Tony Dow should have been given the same benefit and voluntarily gave him 10 percent as well, retroactive to 1957. The old MCA/Universal family management style was like that, from the top on down.

In 1998, our merchandise agreement was renegotiated to include items like videos and CD-Roms. In 1957, we never would have thought that people would still want to buy Beaver Cleaver coffee cups, T-shirts, hats, mouse pads, and more. The forty-year-plus "family" relationship with the studio continues. I have heard horror stories about how actors, writers, directors, and others who worked on shows have been mistreated by studio executives. I have never experienced that with Universal Studios, past or present. Maybe that is why Universal, in all its forms, continues to be so very successful.

So when MCA bought Universal in 1959, *Leave It to Beaver* came along with the package. We had switched from CBS to ABC in 1958 when Purina Dog Chow had become our main sponsor. We remained with ABC through the duration of the show; the last episode aired on September 12, 1963.

There is an interesting sidebar as well. Because the show was sold to ABC instead of NBC, all of the reruns are in black and white. The big color surge was with NBC. If Purina had bought time on NBC instead of ABC, people would be watching the show in color today. But a lot of people *like* the idea that it's in black and white. Although it might not play as well to some of today's kids, it makes very little difference to me one way or the other. If the time comes that they ever colorize it, the purists will still be able to see it in black and white. It's not like taking a black and white painting and painting over it permanently.

I should say something about the quality of education I received at the studio. It was nothing short of excellent. Actually, it was similar to the concept of school in a very small town, where they put four or five grades together. My dad, a professional educator, noted this in his interview with Hal Humphrey: "Actually I believe that Jerry is learning as much or more than he would be getting in normal classroom instruction because this is individual attention. I quiz him periodically, just to be sure."

And he did! I always say that I got an education that most people in the United States couldn't afford. It's like the kings and queens of Europe might have had. We had a private tutor who met with us every day. There were no tests, because the teacher sat there with me and knew exactly what I knew and what I didn't know. So she could take as much time as needed to get me up to speed on each subject. We received three hours of concentrated instruction each day.

As we entered our third season and our first at Universal Studio, the show was very much intact. So now is a good time to mention some of the main ancillary characters and the actors who portrayed them. Beaver's number one cohort and best friend is Larry Mondello, played in the show by Rusty Stevens. Like the Beav, he wears a baseball cap, but he's about forty pounds heavier, weighing in at 114 pounds. His home life is hardly happy. As Larry tells Beaver one day, his father's way of getting to the bottom of things is via direct pressure to Larry's bottom. He is best remembered as the kid who's always digging something out of his pocket to eat. In one episode, Larry's mother bakes a cake for the school bake sale, but Larry eats it before he delivers it. As Wally says, at the Mondello's house "somebody is always eating, and if they're not eating, they're hollerin'."

Beaver's major nemesis is Gilbert Bates. On a good day, Gilbert would make a worthy adversary for Eddie Haskell. A wise guy in miniature, Gilbert was played by Steve Talbot, son of longtime actor Lyle Talbot. Gilbert tells lies, and always tries to tempt Beaver's conscience. Eddie Haskell is ticked because Gilbert is an upstart who threatens Eddie's turf. To Eddie, Gilbert is "hydrant head," a name that evolved because of Gilbert's big ears.

Then we have little Whitey Whitney, played by Stanley Fafara. Whitey's a cute kid whose real name is Hubert and who gets the best grades in school. He's best remembered as the wise guy who got Beaver to climb up into the soup billboard. And there's Richard Rickover, played of course by Rich Correll. Richard, like Gilbert, is always trying to get Beaver to do something he really shouldn't do. He even got a "D" in citizenship for hitting a girl on school property. In his initial appearance on the show, he spills oil on Wally's good suit and gets Beaver to use bleach on the stain, which wrecks the suit completely. It took Eddie Haskell, of all people, to get Beaver out of this jam.

Then there were the girls. I've already mentioned Veronica Cartwright who played Lumpy's sister Violet, and who planted me with my first TV kiss. Mary Ellen Rodgers, played by Pamela Baird, was one of the many Mayfield High girls with eyes for Wally. Pretty and pert, her family lived around the corner from the Cleavers, and she'd had a big crush on Wally since the eighth grade. Her main competition for Wally's affections was the flirtatious Julie Foster played by Cheryl Holdridge.

Judy Hensler was the goody-two-shoes and all purpose tattletale at Grant Elementary School. Played by Jeri Weil, Judy wears iron stiff pigtails to compliment her perpetually sour expression. "Judy's the meanest girl in the world," is Larry Mondello's assessment of her. Few who knew Judy would disagree. Penny Woods and Beaver had a love-hate relationship throughout the series. Blond and stuck-up, she could be as much a terror as Judy Hensler. But she could be a lot nicer too. Neither she nor Beaver minced any words in their verbal sparring. "If her face was on television, her parents wouldn't let little kids watch it," was one of Beaver's favorite admonitions.

But there was one female on the show that Beaver just adored. This was his favorite teacher, Miss Landers. Played by Sue Randall, Beaver had a big crush on her and encouraged Ward and June to invite her over for dinner. Beaver's heart was broken when Miss Landers announced that she was engaged to be married. She remained the essence of patience, sweetness, and kindness for young Beaver Cleaver.

Finally, no cast list would be complete without mentioning Richard Deacon, the bald, bespectacled character actor who played Fred Rutherford, Lumpy and Violet's father. A blowhard with little couth, Fred is Ward's co-worker and self-proclaimed best friend. He's always bragging about his son Clarence to everyone, except when he gets Lumpy alone and mercilessly berates him as a "knucklehead," a "big boob," and a "stupid oaf."

A longtime Hollywood player, usually in comic snoop roles, Richard Deacon had the distinction of being on two hit shows simultaneously. In addition to being Fred Rutherford on *Leave It to Beaver* (1957 to 1963), he also played Mel Cooley on the *Dick Van Dyke Show* from 1961 to 1966.

Add Diane Brewster as Miss Canfield, Beaver's second grade teacher; Doris Packer as Mrs. Cornelia Rayburn, the school principal; Madge Blake as Mrs. Mondello; and Burt Mustin, as Gus the old-timer at the fire station, and we have the cast of characters that allowed *Leave It to Beaver* to enjoy a six-year run on network TV.

chapter 10

These Are a Few of Our Favorite Shows

I watched *Leave It to Beaver* even before I auditioned for the show. It was an institution. Jerry was a very nice kid, and there was that one episode when I had to give him a kiss on the cheek. On another show, I gave him a black eye. Years later, when they did the new show, they brought me back as Violet. It was a lot of fun. They made me into sort of a sex kitten with leather outfits.

—*Veronica Cartwright*

On February 6, 1959, I received one of the great honors of my young life. It was a letter from Mark Hatfield, Governor of the State of Oregon. It read as follows:

WHEREAS, Gerald P. Mathers portrays "Beaver" on the television series *Leave It to Beaver*, and

WHEREAS, the State of Oregon is known as "The Beaver State,"

BE IT HEREBY RESOLVED in this year of the Oregon Statehood Centennial, that

Gerald P. Mathers, better known as the "Beaver," is hereby proclaimed an honorary "Oregonian."

Mark G. Hatfield
GOVERNOR

Moppet Polished Off 30 Licorice Sticks

Little Jerry Mathers put a dent in the budget of Paramount's "The Seven Little Foys." In a scene with Bob Hope, Jerry, who plays Brynie Foy at 5, is seen eating licorice. Propman Earl Olin said he could have all the candy that was left. When Jerry came to collect there wasn't any. In two days he had consumed 30 sticks of licorice.

Courtesy of Jerry Mathers.

Mother, Dad, Susie and me on the lawn in front of our Tarzana house.

Courtesy of Jerry Mathers.

An early calendar shot, this one was for summer.

Courtesy of Jerry Mathers.

My grisly discovery started the action in
The Trouble with Harry with Shirley MacLaine.

Rehearsing with Bob Hope and Eva Marie Saint and on camera with Hope and his son, Kelly, in *That Certain Feeling*.

Photos copyright © 1956 by P. & F. Productions and Hope Enterprises, Inc./Courtesy of Paramount Pictures Corporation.

Once I started working on *Beaver*, the studio
sometimes sent photographers to our house
for shots of the whole Mathers family.

Courtesy of Jerry Mathers.

With Ron-Ton-Ton, the dog who saved our lives.

Photo by Jay Zoerner/Courtesy of Jerry Mathers.

But I wasn't just crazy about dogs; horses, and getting to ride them when we visited my uncle, were also at the top of the list.

Courtesy of Jerry Mathers.

With Hugh Beaumont and Tony Dow. "Dad" instructed us in a variety of masculine arts, like proper use of power tools.

The Universal lot was unbelievable fun for me. I was curious about so many things and was encouraged

... to learn the proper care of a Colt .45 under the tutelage of John Payne.

... to take photographs.

... and to raid the studio newsstand, usually for car magazines.

Shooting wacky water sequences at Friends' Lake and
warming up afterward (note my mom in the background,
keeping a careful eye on my stuntwork).

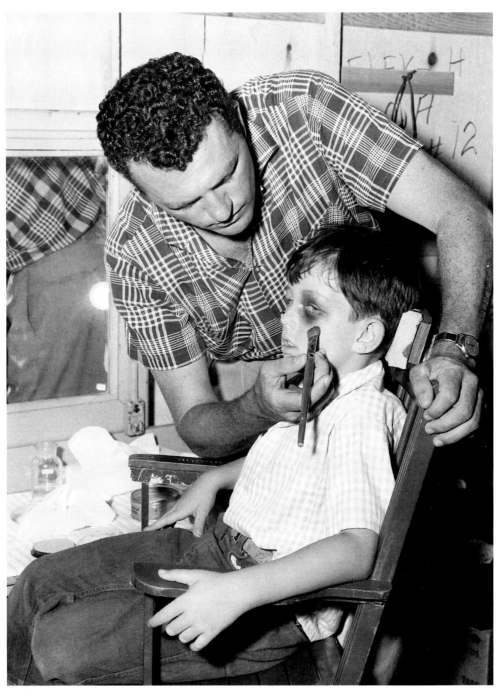

Bob Dawn, our makeup man, loading me up with a pretty realistic-looking shiner.

Miss Landers directed
the Beav's school life . . .

. . . but my real learning as Jerry came
out of this huge trunk of books, which
was always on the set.

And, of course, there was
actual homework. Here I'm
helped by my dad, Norman.

Being an ambassador for the show was great fun, whether it was seeing myself on a comic book . . .

Courtesy of Jerry Mathers.

. . . or going on the road with Tony Dow to promote U.S. Savings Bonds.

Being directed on the kitchen
set by Norman Tokar.

Bob Mosher, accustomed to
writing a daily radio show, loved
having five full days to fine-tune
a *Leave It to Beaver* script.

With Ron-Ton-Ton's successor, Ron-Ton-Two.

Me around the time of Beaver and the Trappers.

The only photo of me in uniform.

Courtesy of Jerry Mathers.

During my stint behind the microphone, not the camera.

Courtesy of Jerry Mathers.

Working with Tony Dow, again, in *Boeing, Boeing*.

Copyright © 1980 by Carder Photography/Courtesy of Jerry Mathers.

And again, in *So Long Stanley*.

Courtesy of Jerry Mathers.

Reunited and added to, in the *New Leave It to Beaver*.

On the original show, Barbara Billingsley never served us lemonade from a tray.

Ken Osmond, Barbara Billingsley, Tony Dow and me pre–Jenny Craig.

Courtesy of Jerry Mathers.

My parents' fiftieth wedding anniversary with the whole extended family.
My daughters, Gretchen and Merci, are in the front row on the right.

Photo by Paul McCallum/Courtesy of Jerry Mathers.

I was so identified by that time as the Beaver that "Jerry Mathers" submerged into a second identity. Even now if I appear on the *Tonight Show* with Jay Leno, it is in some capacity pertaining to the Beaver. Jay Leno has been particularly nice to me in recent years. When there was a lull in my career, he made it a point to have me on his show. He's a good guy and we respect each other a lot. He seems to enjoy the fact that I'm a regular guy because he's one too.

"TV's Eager Beaver" was the title of a May 27, 1958, article in *Look* magazine. "Jerry Mathers is a small fry television star whose eagerness and simplicity and lack of professional guile have made *Leave It to Beaver* the best situation comedy of the year." What had become increasingly clear was that *Leave It to Beaver* was not a children's show, but rather a show about children that appealed to adults. And the viewers responded accordingly. "[A] big asset of the show is young Beaver himself, Jerry Mathers," wrote William Ewald in his *Radio & TV Comment* column. "Generally I find child actors pretty hateful. They are better consigned for study in museums than for entertainment."

Much of the show's charm was Hugh and Barbara. They were able to convey the fact that they could react like any parents afflicted with two normal kids. Our togetherness as a TV family was rarely cloying. There was a real rapport among all cast members and an air of good humor pervaded the show. Hugh himself stressed this point in a 1959 interview with Ron Tepper of the *Los Angeles Times*, who at the time was visiting the set. He asked Hugh to attribute the factors of the show's success. "Mainly," Hugh said, "the avoidance of hokum, a combination of honesty, good writing and never reaching for laughs. Connelly and Mosher also avoid using gimmicks which many series might use when looking for laughs week after week. Instead as the kids have aged, the scripts have grown with them."

Hugh's point is well taken. The scripts did grow to accommodate the growth of the kids. We see this early on in "It's a Small World," the *Heinz '57* pilot, which predated the series. Because most folks have yet to see it in reruns, let's take a closer look at this long forgotten pilot, which established the series.

Wally (Paul Sullivan) and Beaver want a new bike. Their friend Frankie Bennett (Harry Shearer) tells Beaver that the Franklin Milk Company is having a contest. It's quite simple, says Frankie. Collect a thousand milk bottle caps, take them in, and claim a brand-new bike.

Well, the boys work hard and actually come up with the caps. But when they get to the milk company, Mr. Baxter knows nothing of the contest. His secretary, Miss Simms, knows nothing about it either. (Mr. Baxter and Miss Simms are played by a couple of soon-to-be familiar faces: Richard Deacon and Dianne Brewster.) Mr. Baxter calls his superior, Mr. Cochran (Joe Kerns), who has not heard of the contest either. So Cochran tells Baxter to buy a bike for the boys, lest the Franklin Milk Company would look bad.

Wally and Beaver are very happy, but after assembling the bike, they find out there really was no contest. The boys learn about this from their pal Frankie Bennett, who was just giving Beaver "the runaround" (shades of the future Eddie Haskell). Mr. Baxter is sure that the boys had planned a sham, so he retrieves the bike from the boys and leaves in a huff.

When Baxter returns to work, Mr. Cochran calls to tell him that the main office loves the idea of a contest and that he should hurry and get pictures of the winners. As Baxter is heading back to the Cleaver home, Ward (Casey Adams) is explaining to the boys why they can't have the bike. When Mr. Baxter arrives, the boys refuse to accept the bike because Ward told them they couldn't have it under such conditions. Mr. Baxter leaves in a huff all over again.

In the final scene, Ward tells the disappointed boys to go upstairs and change their shirts for dinner. When they finally do, they come down to learn that Ward has bought them a brand-new bicycle.

Again, Connelly and Mosher put great emphasis on honesty and fairness in writing their scripts. The characters do things and there are consequences. They emphasized the ethical meaning of conflict. They wanted to take the side of the children without making the parents look ridiculous. Connelly always felt that rules were usually tougher on kids than their parents.

Beaver may not initiate the things that get him into trouble, but there are still consequences to his actions. He's usually the innocent sitting there saying, "Oh!" And his friends are telling him, "You can do that! You can get away with it! That's fine!" He believes his friends and he gets into an awful lot of trouble along the way.

Or he will be enticed. For example, somebody might say, "If you send us a penny, we'll send you ten records." Beaver says, "Oh, great! For a penny I'll get ten records!" What he doesn't know is that if you send a penny and get ten records, you'll get records for the rest of your life, and you'll have to pay $9 apiece forever.

Or if you lose your money after your father says don't lose your money so you can get a haircut, and you cut your own hair, there are dire consequences. Or if you wrecked your brother's suit and try to hide it, there are consequences to that too.

If you take your father's baseball autographed by Babe Ruth outside to play because your friend says it's only a baseball and you won't hurt it, and then it gets totally wrecked and you try to forge the signature but you don't know how to spell Babe Ruth, your father will probably be awfully mad.

At the same time, the writers were especially aware of the changes modern life had imposed on parent-child relationships. One time Wally is unhappy because the athletic field has been taken over for a dog show. Ward tells him to go somewhere else and play mumblety-peg. Wally retorts: "Dad, if they catch you with a knife nowadays they arrest you."

Connelly and Mosher were critical of the times, even back then. "A boy had more of a chance to be a boy in our generation," Connelly told writer Richard Dyer MacCann in early 1959. "He could cut across a field with a shotgun and be gone all day Saturday. Now he has to hang around his parents, or else he spends the afternoon in a movie house. Believe me, that may be more dangerous than a shotgun."

"Much of the wonderment of childhood is gone," Mosher told MacCann. "The kids tend to know it all—and much too early. Little is left to be discovered in later years, and you can blame TV for part of that."

Mosher found the story "Beaver Runs Away" literally at his own doorstep. One day his daughter decided to disappear. His wife favored letting her stay away to see how she liked it. Fortunately, they learned she was having dinner with a neighbor and they could afford to wait it out. A few weeks later, a script began to take shape where Beaver stalks out just before dinner after a family misunderstanding. This time it's his dad who lets him do it, much to his regret. Though it turned out that the Beaver was eating heartily at a friend's house.

An episode called "The Garage Painters," which aired in February 1959, always intrigued me. It begins when the TV set is broken and Ward tells the boys that they should read Mark Twain's classic *The Adventures of Tom Sawyer*. Needless to say, the boys are less than enthusiastic. But once they start reading they like it enough to keep on reading. In fact, they keep reading it in bed, using a flashlight under the covers. Here the plans of the parents exceed all their expectations.

Then Mark Twain's book is put to a practical test. When Ward is called to a Saturday meeting, the boys decide to paint the garage. When the other guys come over to watch, they offer no assistance at all. Neither Lumpy nor Larry accepts the bait— they've tried painting before and as far as they're concerned, it's nothing. Only little Benji Bellamy is interested. A can of green paint pours over Benji, and Benji's mother is horrified and blames Beaver and Wally for painting her son. Rather than ending the episode here, this sets up Connelly and Mosher's main idea. June wonders whether it had been wise to take "Tom Sawyer" down from the shelf. Ward feels that books are so important that you always must take a chance, even if it means that little Benji is now green.

The show on alcoholism is particularly interesting. Ward hires an alcoholic painter who comes to paint the house. Ward and June go away for the day, and the painter approaches Beaver for something to drink because it's so hot outside. Beaver tells him he'll get him some lemonade. "Don't you have anything else?" the painter asks. Beaver tells him that Aunt Martha gave his dad something else. So he brings the painter a little bottle of brandy, and the painter gets absolutely soused. When Ward comes home he has to explain to the boys the sad truth that there are some people who just can't drink.

Another episode, called "Beaver and Chuey," dealt with international relationships. Beaver has a friend who's an exchange student who speaks Spanish. Beav asks Eddie Haskell if he knows how to speak Spanish. He says he does, but he's only taken the level one course. Beaver asks, "How do I tell this guy that I want him to be my best friend, Eddie?" Eddie says to please his friend with a certain Spanish phrase; "*Tu fienes cara como pverco.*"

So Beaver repeats Eddie's phrase, which really is, "You have a face like a pig." Chuey runs away crying, and Beaver can't understand why the kid gets all upset. After proper amends are made (but not before also telling Chuey's mother she has a face like a pig), Beaver says that if he's going to be like Eddie when he grows up, he doesn't think he wants to *get* big.

Those are just some of the topics that weren't being dealt with on any other situation comedy—divorce, cultural barriers, and alcoholism. Many TV shows deal with them now, and not as well. This way was very subtle and more effective. Beaver learns at an early age that there are people who are alcoholics. He learns that it is better to tell the truth from the beginning, than to try to lie and hide something bad you might have done. Because when all is said and done you'll get caught.

The one episode that people seem to remember most is the teacup show. Actually it's a soup cup, and the episode was called "In the Soup," but everybody associates it with a teacup. It's the show I'm asked about most often.

It was the most expensive *Leave It to Beaver* we ever did. Normally, the show was budgeted at about $30,000 to $40,000 per episode. Today, a really cheap show is $750,000 to $1,000,000 for a half hour show. But in those days, $30,000 was a big budget show. *Leave It to Beaver* wasn't cheap. But they decided to go way out for this show, and audiences loved it.

At the urging of Whitey Whitney, Beaver gets stuck in a soup bowl on top of a billboard sporting the brand name Zesto

Soups. They actually built two billboards, one outside and the other on the soundstage. The show cost about $50,000. It was a very interesting show, and to answer the most asked question, yes I did all the climbing myself.

The fun part about that was they had to get special permission for me to miss school. It took a week to shoot the whole thing, so my school time was cut short. I had to go an hour the week before for three days, and an hour the week after for three days.

Another favorite episode is "Wally, the Lifeguard." Wally thinks he's getting a job at Friend's Lake as a lifeguard. But when he gets there he finds that he's under the minimum age to be a lifeguard, so he accepts a job selling candy, soda pop, and hot dogs. He has to go around carrying a big bucket of candy.

The whole family goes to the lake thinking he's going to be a big lifeguard. Beaver brags to all his friends that his big brother is a lifeguard. When he discovers that Wally's a walking soda jerk, he's angry because he thinks Wally let him down. But Ward points out that it was Beaver who actually let Wally down, because it was Beaver who tried to look like a big shot to his friends, and it was Wally who caught the bad break.

Friend's Lake is a huge lake on the Universal back lot. It's part of the Universal tour, right above where *Jaws* was filmed. When we were shooting there, during lunch hour Tony and I were allowed to fish in the lake. Universal stacked it with lots of blue gill to eat the mosquitoes. To make hooks, we took straight pins and bent them. Then we'd get tree limbs and string from the prop men, and we'd use bread from the caterer, which we'd roll up into little balls and use for bait. When the blue gills got hungry, they'd jump up and eat the bait. We'd catch lots of fish.

Whenever we went on location it was a big thing. We loved to go to the back lot so we could go to the lake and fish. During "Wally, the Lifeguard," I remember I caught more fish than Tony, and I caught the biggest fish either of us ever caught. To catch more fish than Tony was a real feather in my cap, because he was an older kid and they were supposed to be better than us.

We were allowed to fish for only an hour during our lunch break. And we had to be very careful not to get our shirts wet.

Friend's Lake was supposed to be 50 to 60 miles from Mayfield, and it was one of the Cleavers' favorite vacation spots. It provides the setting for one of Tony Dow's favorite *Leave It to Beaver* episodes.

Tony Dow remembers:

> Perhaps the episode I enjoyed most was one of Norman Tokar's scripts. Ward wanted to take the family camping. He had rented a cottage at Friend's Lake, because when he was a kid that's where he most liked to go. Of course, the boys weren't too excited about it. They wanted to go to the movies. June didn't have anything to wear, and it was a real hassle getting the family together.
>
> They finally go there and nobody is having a good time. Ward is trying to recapture his youth. The guys go fishing and catch a bunch of fish. But it turns out that the pond is stocked and they have to pay for the fish that they catch. So that's disappointing.
>
> Then the cabin isn't as comfortable as Ward had remembered, and he starts feeling that he shouldn't have gone back. He's disappointed. Then the following evening they get ready to leave and Ward can't find the boys. June tells him that they went out a couple of hours earlier. He gets excited and goes out looking for them. He finds them on the top of a hill with a pair of binoculars looking down at something.
>
> He thinks the boys are looking for wildlife. But it turns out that they are watching a drive-in movie that they've seen three times before. Some of the scenes in that episode are really terrific.
>
> There are some other moments I think were great. There is a scene where Wally and Beaver are supposed to take a bath before dinner. They go through the whole ritual of filling the tub. They never once get near the tub. They never once get near that bath. In ritualistic manner,

Wally gets the washcloths and dumps them in three times and puts some soap on them. Beaver takes the towels and lays them out. He makes them damp.

They are talking about something totally unrelated. But you know that they do this every night. This is how they take their bath. Then they crumble the towels up and throw them in the corner. As they start out the door, Wally reaches in the Beaver's jacket, pulls out some dirt, throws it in the bathtub, and says, "It will leave a ring."

The shows were remarkable. The camping show's statement is that you can't go back. They were subtle, they were understated. Just when you thought the boys were finally enjoying themselves, they put in a twist and they are watching a movie.

My very favorite episode is "The Lying Down Horse." I know that it's one of Barbara Billingsly's favorites too. It was the first episode that Hugh Beaumont actually wrote and directed, and like the song says, everything that could go wrong really did go wrong.

It's the story of how Wally and the Beaver go to work at the circus. Wally and the Beaver go to the circus to shovel straw. The circus doesn't want one of its horses because it only lies down, so instead of getting paid, they bring the horse home and keep it in the garage. Hugh wrote it because he had actually heard that there was a horse that could lay down on command.

We were under very strict time constraints and had to finish the show in five days. We bring the horse in and start shooting the scene with the horse in the garage. It was a real good horse, and he's just standing there calm as can be. When we get to the point where the trainer gives the horse the sign to lay down, the horse doesn't move. He steadfastly refuses.

They paid all this money for a trick horse that lays down on command and he won't do a thing. They continue to try: a half hour, forty-five minutes, an hour, and the horse still refuses. Now they're way behind schedule and getting another horse is out of the question, so they decide to get a vet and tranquilize the horse.

The vet arrives and gives the horse a shot of tranquilizers. Nothing happens. The horse is stimulated now, perhaps because he's on a TV set. So the vet gives him another shot of tranquilizers. Well, the horse just goes crazy. He bucks and his legs start kicking and he knocks down the walls of the garage. Since the sets are just walls, we can't shoot in the garage anymore because the horse has knocked down the set. It will take a day to rebuild the garage. The tranquilizers are taking hold and the horse is finally lying down now and they can't move it.

Now we are so far behind schedule that we have to go into the living room. We decide to do a scene, but nobody knows the lines because it wasn't supposed to be shot until the next day. But because we have to make up time, we go in there and start shooting. As soon as we begin, the horse who is fast asleep starts farting. So every time we are halfway through the scene, he starts at it again. Well, now we can't shoot again for the rest of the day. Poor Hugh Beaumont. This is his first writing and directing job on the show and he's in big trouble because he picked the wrong thing to write about.

On October 3, 1959, *Leave It to Beaver* began its third season, and its second with ABC. Entitled "Blind Date Committee," the premier episode of the 1959–1960 season was directed by Norman Tokar and written by Katherine and Dale Eunson as well as Connelly and Mosher. The episode featured Beverly Washburn as Jill, a new girl in town who needs a date for the dance. A fine actress, Beverly had stirred everyone's hearts two years earlier in the 1957 Disney favorite, *Old Yeller.*

The year and the decade were winding down fast. Our show was well received in all viewing quarters, and it seemed that everyone knew the Beaver. Our reviews were good and getting better. Beaver and Wally were growing up right in front of your TV screens. Jerry Mathers and Tony Dow had added a couple of years on their own frames as well. Tony was an incredibly good looking fourteen-year-old boy—a heartthrob on and off the screen. I had recently celebrated my 12th birthday, and was readily anticipating becoming a real live teenager like Tony. My vital statistics provided by ABC Television read: height, 4'9"; weight, 85 lbs; hair, brown; eyes, blue.

Leave It to Beaver had set a new refreshing tone for situation comedies, and we did it by celebrating the themes of wit, warmth, and wisdom.

I was made an honorary Oregonian by the State's Governor Mark Hatfield. I had gone to Washington, D.C., under the auspices of the U.S. Treasury Department to accept a Treasury Award on behalf of the *Beaver* show. The award was in recognition of services rendered to the Department by the producers and cast of the show, who recently turned out a special film promoting Savings Bonds. Then to top off everything, Patty McCormick and I were named the top male and female child actors of 1959. To paraphrase from a song Frank Sinatra would sing a few years later, 1959 had been "A Very Good Year."

chapter 11
Winding Down

I was about eleven or twelve years old when we would watch the reruns of *Leave It to Beaver*. Although I was acting and involved in show business, we lived in a working-class neighborhood in Burbank, and *Leave It to Beaver* was a neighborhood staple. After school, we might be playing army, touch football, or something else. Yet when 3:30 came around, everybody would say, "Beaver! Beaver!" And we just knew that it was time to break up and watch the show.

—*Ron Howard*

Although our network switch to ABC in 1958 remained intact, we did have four time changes during the ensuing years. From October 1958 to June 1959, we appeared on Thursday from 7:30 to 8:00 P.M. During the summer of 1959, reruns were aired at 9:00 P.M. on Thursdays. From October 1959 through September 1962, the show aired at 8:30 P.M. on Saturday. Finally during the 1962–1963 season, the show returned to Thursday night, this time at 8:30 P.M.

Our fourth season premiered on Saturday, October 1, 1960. Most of the gang was present: Ken Osmond as Eddie Haskell, Stanley Fafara as Whitey, Stephen Talbot as Gilbert, Frank Bank as Lumpy, Richard Correll as Richard, Jerry Weil as Judy Hensler, and Sue Randall as Miss Landers. Directed by the talented Norman Abbott, who would do the bulk of our show for the final three years, and with General Electric joining Ralston Purina as the main sponsors, the episode was called "Beaver Won't Eat." Beaver's refusal to eat his brussels sprouts at dinner soon leads to punishment and problems. Beaver hated his brussels sprouts, but after managing to ingest one at a restaurant with some help from a back pat by Wally, Beaver finally realizes that his parents were only insisting he eat his sprouts for his own good.

In September 1960, with the approach of our fourth season, Hugh Beaumont wrote an open letter to the American television viewer. In this letter, Hugh touches on many issues, and it bears looking at for merit and content, as well as an indicator of what our show always strived to be. So much of what he saw back then is compounded many times over today:

> One of the most gratifying rewards in life is to have your work appreciated. I'd like to thank you now for the support that is putting *Leave It to Beaver* back on the air for our fourth season. It's particularly gratifying to read your letters of approval at a time when television in general is taking quite a mauling from its detractors.
>
> I know all of us as parents wish there was more good taste on television. Some nights our television sets literally seem to explode with violence, sudden death, brutality and an overemphasis on sex.
>
> Just where does the responsibility for our programming lie? True, some of it lies with the television industry but television doesn't create a culture—it caters to a culture. If producers and the networks think this is what you want, this is what you're going to get.
>
> We who have children realize what a tremendous influence television has on the young. From television, they often pick their heroes. How does this affect them if their hero solves his problems with violence? Or their favorite comedian gets a laugh by spitting out a mouthful of food?
>
> We know the influence that *Leave It to Beaver* has on children from the letters we get from parents. One man recently told us that his boy wouldn't have thought of pulling out his chair for his mother at dinner till he saw it happen on the *Beaver* show. We get lots of letters from

teachers—it's one of the few shows they urge their pupils to watch.

To us, things like helping mother with the dishes, wearing a jacket or tie on a date . . . are more than just surface attributes—we think of them as symbols of respect.

If a child doesn't respect his parents and his teachers, he'll end up respecting nothing, not even himself.

We don't presume to claim that *Leave It to Beaver* and shows like it will save the world, or even revolutionize television. But we do make an honest effort to present an honest and moral view of family life here in America.

As long as you and people like you pick out what is good in television, and let us know about it, the producers will be encouraged to give you more shows that respect good taste and moral values. It's up to you to change television before it changes you.

Of course, *Leave It to Beaver* presented an idealistic picture of life. Ward and June were skilled parents who dressed neatly and rarely fought with one another. And certainly no set of family problems can be solved within the time constraints of thirty minutes, less the necessary allotment for commercial breaks. But we must remember, though this was only a TV show, it was one which was designed to reflect what was best in family life across the land.

Nor should anyone dismiss the show's realities. Here Tony Dow and Barbara Billingsly share their own insights.

Tony Dow:

I disagree with those who say that the Cleavers weren't real, because Mom vacuumed in high heels and Dad wore a suit and tie to dinner. There was a formality for lots of people in the 1950s. Many people followed that mold. For example, I never saw Joe Connelly and Bob Mosher without a shirt and tie. Even though my family did not particularly subscribe to this, there were certainly many families who did.

There was a relationship between the parents and the kids, the parents to each other, and the kids to each other. Wally was a transitional character between the parents and Beaver. In terms of reality, I think the stories are so real and the problems we dealt with are so universal and so true, that everybody can find things to identify with and emulate. The magic words here are Truth and Honesty.

The first year Jerry and I were in school together. Then we had our own teachers. But we used to play ball together. An interesting thing about the show was we'd go play basketball and our shirts would become sweaty and would be hanging out. We'd go do the scene and all the grass stains on our knees were from playing basketball. They let us be real kids. It had that added texture that you don't get to see today.

We grew up first at Revue and then at Universal. The back lot was our playground. So we had other kids there. We'd play a game of football in the middle of Laramie Street. Or we'd play a game of hide-and-seek.

Barbara Billingsly:

When you look at *Leave It to Beaver* now, and you look at some of the sitcoms today, there is no comparison. The writing, the honesty of it is missing. They keep looking at Beaver today. I get letters from all over. It's really something. Why do many men tell me that I was their second mom?

When they complain that I dressed too well, I reply that a lot of the clothes came from Penney's. They're not expensive clothes. Once in a while I had on a good sweater. My mother always wore high heels. But on the show, I *only* wore high heels to be taller than the boys. I started off in flats. If you ever see my feet in the early shows when the kids are little, I'm wearing low heels. As the boys grew, I began wearing high heels.

I remember some episodes better than others. The

episode with the soup will always stand out. So will the episode with the horse. Jerry was terrified with the horse. They bring the horse home and put it in the garage, but June and Ward don't know about it. They have to have a vet come and put it to sleep. Before they put it to sleep, Jerry ran across the stage, ran into the living room of the house, and fell over the sofa. He was terrified.

So they put this horse to sleep, then after they shot the scene they couldn't wake him up. We did our close-ups after dark when the boys went home. It was pitch-dark and there were four men and they got this horse propped up. And every time somebody would leave the horse would go sinking down. And it spoiled more takes because it snored. That was the funniest thing that happened.

On one show, Jerry gave me a blouse with the Eiffel Tower on it. He insisted that I wear it to school for the PTA meeting. It was a very cute episode. After the show was over, I didn't see Jerry as much as I saw Tony, because Tony and I worked together as adults. I got to know Jerry better when we did the *New Leave It to Beaver* series in Florida at the new Universal Studios. He's a very considerate and nice person.

Tony was really a big brother to Jerry on the show. He would take Jerry out when he had a car. I just can't believe it's been forty years now, but it is. How fortunate to have been a part of all this. If I had to be in any show, my goodness, it couldn't have been a better show. Most people think we have a classic. I think so too.

If I had wanted to do other things like Tony Dow and even Hugh, then perhaps being June Cleaver might have been a detriment to my career. But being well known for one part has been wonderful to me because I have done so many other things as a result of it. Even my stint in *Airplane* I did because I was June Cleaver.

I think they create a character and as the show goes on the character evolves. I certainly don't see June Cleaver as a wimp as some people do. There are several episodes where she really separates the boys. She doesn't say in a whiny voice like Mrs. Mondello, "Just you wait until your father gets home." I often say that Hugh was the law and I was the love.

I see no reason why the woman couldn't have a little excitement in her life too. They didn't have a bedroom, but possibly there was something else going on there. We came out of a door. If we were called and had to leave the bedroom at night, we had a door. We had our robes on when we came out. Jerry likes to recall how we couldn't even say the word "pregnant" back then.

Again, so many people tell me I was their second mother. It doesn't matter if the person is black or white, they still have the same feeling. Everyone would like to come home from school and find Mom there. They'd like to have Mom there. *I absolutely believe that.*

In many ways, women's lib has been the worst thing that has happened to the family. In the workplace, yes! Whatever they do they should be paid equal amount to men. But they have just lost the way men and women feel about each other. I happen to like men. And that awful thing of suing if a man looks at you! Hell's bells, I was flattered.

June Cleaver was a great mom because a woman will never have a better job in her whole life than mothering a child. Because believe me, you will reap great problems if you don't do a good job. My mother worked, but she spent her whole life when she wasn't working with her children. I always made it a policy to do the same.

At eleven I became the first youngster to start a new College Club Account with the North Hollywood Federal Savings. Even as a pre-teen riding the wave of success as a young actor, I never expected to be an actor all my life, and I felt the College Club would be a worthy investment for my future. I never doubted that I would go to college one day, and investing at least $5 a week at dividends of 4 percent would one day be enough to pay for an entire four-year college career. There were also the Coogan Laws.

When Tony and I signed with Gomalco Productions, the judge ordered that each of us set aside 15 percent of our earnings for savings. Two years later, the judge called us into his chamber to ask if we would increase our savings to 20 percent. My dad and Tony's mother were both at the hearing. My dad told the judge that he too had been matching my savings, was planning to invest the money, and asked the judge to keep our forced savings at 15 percent. Mureal Dow, Tony's mother, also assured Judge Clark that she had a similar plan for Tony.

If there is one thing I would recommend to young performers today it is to provide for your future by saving, especially for college. The entertainment business always has been fickle, and it's more fickle and transitory now than ever before. The fall from stardom can be painful and destructive for anyone, that's why the casualty rate—emotional and physical—has been great for so many child actors. The best advice I can offer is to develop other interests and endeavors while you're still on top.

I was fortunate to have a loving and stable family life behind the decisions I made. One of the most important decisions was the one to leave show business on my own. Universal was not about to unload me just because the show came to an end—they were already promising me other work. Moreover, my parents allowed me to make my own decision. They neither tried to persuade nor dissuade me.

I had other interests. I wanted to play baseball and high school football like the other guys. Remember, my father was a coach and most Friday evenings were spent in the stands watching his teams perform. I had even thought about becoming a lawyer or a career law enforcement officer one day. I just hungered to be one of the guys. I wanted to follow in my dad's footsteps and become a part of Notre Dame High School.

All three Mathers children had touched the show business arena. Susie was still modeling and doing occasional TV shows. My brother Jimmy did *Ichabod and Me* for Connelly and Mosher, and he continued acting throughout the 1960s.

Each summer my mom and dad would pack the three kids

into a car and journey somewhere on vacation. We always drove—we were a middle American family. Twice we visited my dad's family in Iowa, one time the summer before the show, and once while we were doing the show.

Although Susie and I had both appeared in pictures, when we first went back to Iowa in 1957 it was my dad the family made a fuss over. Norm Mathers had been a star athlete in Sioux City years before—a hometown boy. The radio stations were after him. There were huge family picnics each summer. No one had expected to have a slice of show business in the family.

On another vacation, we visited Hugh Beaumont in Minnesota. Hugh's wife was from the state and he had bought an island there. We had a great few days on water skis and playing with Hugh and Kathryn's kids. Susie got leeches wading in the lake and Hugh, the arid sportsman, burned them off with a cigarette. It also gave my mother a chance to see some of her relatives. My folks had become quite friendly with Hugh and Kathryn Beaumont as a result of the show.

The funny thing about my TV fame is that I was more popular outside Los Angeles than I was here at home. It's still that way today. The further we got from L.A., the more I was recognized. When I'd get to New York, I met more fans than anywhere else.

Another summer we drove to Oregon, Washington, and into Canada. There was a little town in Oregon that had a comer restaurant with three little stools. There was a man sitting next to me. He said, "You look very much like that little boy on TV." I said, "I am!" I loved seeing how surprised he was.

Another interesting family story was set at a motel in Oregon. My sister Susie met up with a little girl right away. They were playing and having all kinds of fun, when the little girl's mother called out to her. "[Linda], the Beaver's on!" The little girl said to Susie, "Oh, I can't play with you. *Leave It to Beaver* is on! See you later!"

If there's anyone in the family who knows and understands the trials and tribulations of being a child actor, it's my brother Jimmy. After all, he's been in the industry himself in one capacity or another for more than three decades and works with young actors today.

Jimmy Mathers told me recently:

> I always really looked up to my brother Jerry. I was always real proud of him and I still am. I wanted to be like him as a little boy. Ever since I could remember he had been an actor and a television star. That's one part of our relationship. Another part is that I felt sorry for him over the years. I had the benefit of doing a little bit of acting, which was a lot of fun. But I was never a star. I could go off and do a job. I could do a movie for a couple of months, or an episode for a TV show for a week, and be back with my friends. Nobody would recognize me. I feel sorry in a way that until high school, Jerry was robbed of having a regular childhood.
>
> But Jerry never showed the fame. I always thought, even during his glory days, that all he wanted to do was to be a regular guy. And deep down he is. When the show was over he went to public (Parochial) school. It wasn't a private school for famous kids. Then later he went to the University of California at Berkeley. But it was the kind of thing that *nobody wanted to leave him alone.* He was the Beaver! He's been smart to protect his image over all these years. He's been offered a lot of money to do things he would not do.

We opened our fifth season on September 30, 1961, with an episode called "Wally Goes Steady" directed by Norman Abbott. Ward and June fear that Wally may be lured into marriage by an eager girlfriend named Evelyn. Also in the cast was a young actor named Ryan O'Neal who a few years later would achieve stardom as Rodney Harrington in the TV series *Peyton Place.*

I was thirteen years old now and had been in front of a camera for more than ten years. I was developing new interests and new hobbies every day. Moreover, I was growing taller and was beginning to get a typical adolescent's complexion. TV was changing too. During our next to last season we ran into some stiff competition from *The Defenders*, starring E. G. Marshall and Robert Reed. The following year it was *Perry Mason* and *Dr. Kildare*.

My brother Shaun was born in March, 1963. In May, we filmed the final episode of *Leave It to Beaver* to be aired in September. I continued to go to school at Universal for three hours a day until the end of the school year in June. With the birth of Shaun, my mother had another full-time job. And when my brother Patrick was born twenty-one months later in 1965, it became a double duty job for her.

While Susie and Jimmy had never remembered a time when I wasn't in front of the camera, Shaun and Patrick came around after their oldest brother was out of the spotlight. In fact, when Shaun was in the second grade, around 1970, he was placed in the advanced classes. One day he came home from school and told my mom that a friend said that his brother Jerry was a celebrity who had been on TV for years. He never knew I had been a famous TV star until that day. My mother always said that in real life I was never really like the Beaver, that Shaun and Patrick were actually more like the character I played on TV than I was: "I stayed home and it was like living through the Beaver. They would do the things and stuff that Beaver actually did on the air."

The final *Leave It to Beaver* episode was titled "Family Scrapbook." June was cleaning out the cabinets, and she finds a long forgotten scrapbook of family pictures. She calls Ward and the boys, and the four start reminiscing over incidents which are brought to life with flashbacks that spring from the photos they flip through.

These golden family moments included Beaver discussing his first note from school with Wally, as the two brothers pretend to take a bath. We see the night that Miss Landers came over for dinner. "Little girls don't smell as nice as you do," Beaver says when Miss Landers suggests that one day Beaver will find a nice little girl his own age. (Through the whole program we never learned Miss Landers' first name.)

We see and relive Wally's first attempt at shaving, and the time that Beaver ran away. We meet a young Eddie Haskell talking about his first girlfriend. We watch Wally as he campaigns for class president, and Mary Ellen Rogers' ploy to woo Wally by appealing to his taste for doughnuts.

Leave It to Beaver was not renewed for the 1963–1964 season. Connelly and Mosher were busy at work with *The Munsters,* their new television series, but that was not the real reason. They were prolific enough to do two shows. The truth is that time had simply run out for Wally and Beaver. They were growing up. To this day, Joe Connelly feels that it's because we decided to call it quits when we did that the series has endured so well. I agree. We never overplayed our hand. Wally and Beaver left TV with their physical presence intact and their youthful faces forever imprinted into lasting lore.

chapter 12
High School Days

There's no message or speech, but you know that when the story ends, America underwent a drastic change. The early '60s was the end of an era. It hit us all very hard.

—*George Lucas to the* New York Times, *on his film* American Graffiti

F or some people, their high school years were truly happy days. For others, these years were mired by uncertainty and doubt. Most people find something of both to cling to. But rarely are these years viewed entirely with indifference.

My generation of young Americans was beautifully captured on screen in the 1973 film *American Graffiti*. Few films have shown as warmly and humanly the eagerness, the joys, the sadness, and the sorrows of a generation of kids soon to lose their innocence. In the film there's a scene where one of the guys wraps a logging chain around the back of a police car. When the police pull out fast, the chain rips out the back axle of the police car. That scene was taken from a scene in *Leave It to Beaver*, when to get back at Lumpy Rutherford, Wally and Eddie put a logging chain around a tree and wrap it to the back of Lumpy's 1940 Ford convertible.

When I entered Notre Dame High School in the fall of 1963, it was with anticipation tempered by an appropriate degree of trepidation. Remember, in spite of all my talk of wanting to be a regular guy, my formative years to date had been in show business, and all my formal schooling had taken place inside the gates of a giant movie studio. Beaver Cleaver was no more. I was fifteen-year-old Jerry Mathers, a high school freshman, and I was embarking on unfamiliar turf.

But I wasn't totally unprepared. I spent most of the summer of 1963 with the Marine Reserves in Camp Pendleton, California. It was a great experience and one that most certainly prepared me for that proverbial real world out there.

As a kid I had always wanted to be a Marine. So during the summer, my dad was able to put me in a program with the Marine Reserves, feeling that it could really toughen me up. His reasoning was sound. He thought it would be a good idea for me to be toughened up in case anybody gave me trouble for being an actor. The deal was that the Marine Reserves would take mostly underprivileged kids and put them through a tough summer program. One of the coaches at my dad's school said they took other kids too, including some kids from his football team. So he worked it out that I could go too.

In the summer of 1963 it was off to Camp Pendleton. When we arrived, the first thing they did was shave our heads. We were placed in barracks and lived just like Marine recruits, with a Marine Reserve member as a drill sergeant. It was just like real military training and I loved it. We had recreational boxing. I loved guns and was able to train on the M1 rifle. They took us out on the range, and you better believe we were all crack shots by summer's end. At the end of the program, each platoon nominated a best "recruit." I was nominated from my platoon and became one of the five or six finalists. Someone else won the award, but I was thrilled to get as far as I did.

My main passions in high school were sports and music. I tried out and made both the freshman and the junior varsity football squads, and I organized my first rock group called Beaver and the Trappers. One of the original members of Beaver and the Trappers was my old friend Richard Correll.

Rich went to a prep school in San Jose for a year before transferring to Loyola. But different schools never ended our relationship. Our high school years, in fact, found us growing closer. So although Rich and I went to different high schools, he dated a lot of the girls I knew, and I dated a lot of the girls he knew. I was even with Richard the very first time he kissed a girl. It was in Disneyland, and I had a Silver 1964 GTO, which I thought was really cool. The car had good power, and I was a pretty good driver. Rich would sit in the backseat with his girl next to him. I would sit in the driver's seat with my date next to me. It really *was* like *American Graffiti*.

The prevailing credo for many kids during the 1960s was "sex, drugs and rock 'n' roll." In fact it has falsely become a tag line for our entire generation. Yet for us the only one of the three carnal pleasures we truly enjoyed was "rock 'n' roll."

It really paid off having a cute younger sister like Susie as a high school kid. My group of friends started hanging out with Susie's group of friends. In fact, Rich and Susie became very good friends and remain so today. Rich and I would have what we called "Richard and Jerry Parties." Because we were in the same band, we'd bring a bass player and maybe one other guy, and tell the girls that we wanted to have a party. Thirty girls would show up, and we were only four guys.

Richard Correll remembers them well:

> You couldn't believe—this being the sixties—how clean these parties were. No booze. No dope. No nothing! We sat around and sang songs. We would play them too. Everybody loved The Beatles. Everybody loved The Stones, The Beach Boys, The Byrds. For the girls it was like having a jukebox, only it was all live. And, of course, we were in heaven. There were thirty-one girls and just us.
>
> We started having parties over at one of the guys' house, who was also a singer. His name was Charlie Wick. We called him C. Z. Wick. C. Z. lived next door to me when we were kids. It was another huge house, and Jerry and I would go there and show movies. We started with thirty people. Then it was sixty people. The next time it was ninety people. C. Z. had his own private screening room. We'd run horror movies and the girls

would all cuddle up because they were afraid. We had it made. These parties were really great.

The point that I'm making is that even in the later part of the 1960s, we kept things clean. A lot of parents were just amazed that so many kids could get together, completely unchaperoned and high school age, and not be up to something. Nobody was getting stoned. Nobody was getting drunk, nobody was trying to get into somebody else's pants. It was really a good group of kids. I've always said that if I was writing a script for a sitcom today, nobody would believe it.

Jerry and I were always up to things. I can remember one time Jerry was taking a girl to a prom. It was black tie and it was at the Beverly Hills Hotel. My father had a black Cadillac, but it wasn't my car. Jerry said, "I got this great idea. I can really impress this girl if I get picked up in a limo. But since I can't afford a limo, I want to see if you can get your father's car and pick me up in it." So I told my dad that I really had to use his car. He said okay, but the car had to be home by midnight. So Jerry and I planned this big scheme. I got this thin tie, a white shirt, a black jacket, and a chauffeur's hat. I pretended that I didn't know him. So we picked up this girl and everything was great, great, great. We took her to the prom, and he was acting like a big shot. She was so impressed.

When I dropped him off I said, "Okay Mr. Mathers, have a good time. I'll come and get you!" He said, "Thank you. Come and get me at 1:30!" I went, "Hmmmmm, well, I've got a bit of a problem here. I've got to get this car back by midnight!" "You can't do this to me," Jerry said. "You got to pick me up. I got to be picked up!" I said, "Okay, I'll think of something." I did! I picked him up in something like a 1960 Chevy, a totally different car, broken down. I had to think really fast. So I told him and his date that I had mechanical problems, and this was the only car I could *rent*. You know the girl liked him so much that she bought it. She completely bought it!

Being a red-blooded young man, my attention was veering more and more toward the opposite sex. When I entered my junior year, I started dating a number of girls. But my first real girlfriend was Jeanne Roach, Hal Roach's daughter. Hal Roach, of course, was one of the great producers of his day. He teamed with Harold Lloyd, and he later made films with Our Gang and Laurel and Hardy as well as making lots of high-quality talking pictures.

I met Jeanne when a bunch of us were playing co-ed touch football at UCLA. We dated through most of my junior year and all of my senior year. I took her to my senior prom, and even to the Emmys, when I gave the award to Gene Kelly for Best Childrens' Program of 1967. But like so many high school romances, eventually geography took its toll. After high school, I went into the service and she went away to college. I totally lost track of her, but I did see a picture of her in the paper a few years ago, when Hal Roach died at the age of 100.

But I never lost touch with Richard Correll. Our friendship, which started way back on the set of Universal Studios, got stronger and stronger.

Earlier, I mentioned how Rich would visit me in Canoga Park and how sad he was when he had to go home. The ironic thing about this was that Rich was probably the richest person I knew. He had butlers and maids. In fact, the family had two cooks, five gardeners, two butlers, and two maids. And as much as he wanted to come to my house, I *loved* to go to his house. Because at Rich's, I was treated like a little king—the servants would do everything for me. Rich's parents were both very busy and traveled a lot, so the kids had nannies to watch over them. When I went to dinner at Rich's house, it was always formal and I had to dress in a shirt and tie. And I had to wash up for dinner—and not just my hands. Rich's mother would ring a little bell and a maid and butler would bring out the different courses.

So here's a kid who had a maid who would make his bed and pick up his clothes. And he had a cook who let him order whatever he wanted to eat. But he loved our house. Maybe it was more fun to "mess around" in a more casual atmosphere. He liked the family thing at our house, where we would have a big dinner that my grandmother and mother would cook. My father would pass the food around and everybody would just dig in.

Richard had a pipeline of sorts to the rich and famous. One day Rich got a call from a wealthy woman who wanted to invite the two of us to a party. She said there were going to be a lot of young people at the party and that we'd just love it.

Well, it ended up being a fund-raiser for Richard Nixon. We went there only because we thought there would be lots of pretty girls. I had just bought a motorcycle, but Richard didn't think I was too adept at driving it. So when I told Rich that I wanted him to ride on the back of the motorcycle, he gave me some flimsy excuse. The truth is, he thought I'd kill him.

We went to the party and there were a couple of very pretty girls, one who was hanging all over me. She was the kind of girl whom Rich labelled a "bombshell." As luck would have it, she also had a friend who was rather homely and uninteresting, and she wouldn't go anywhere without her friend. So I appealed to Rich. "Hey, hey, hey, come on! You've got to help me out. You've got to take this other girl!" Rich kept saying, "No! No! Absolutely not!" So I told him that I'd take both of the girls on the back of my motorcycle. Rich got real nervous—full of fear and despair thinking of the three of us on a motorcycle.

I went out to start the motorcycle. The girls were hanging on to me, and the motorcycle began to sway from side to side. Richard started to think that if he didn't take the homely girl with him, he'd never see his good pal Jerry again. That I'd be dead—hit by a truck on the next block. Well, Rich got stuck with the homely girl. I took off with the pretty one. As he's said many times since: "It's all in the friend helping a friend category."

Richard Correll corroborates:

The first real big heavy romance I had was Anita Montalbon. She was the daughter of Ricardo Montalbon and the first girl I ever kissed. I was a junior in high school and kind of shy. Jerry was always giving me pointers, so they must have worked.

I was invited to a party by a girl who was to become

the big romance of my life. Her name was Carol Lohman. It was one of those sight unseen things. Her father, an oil real estate man from Texas, had been in business with my dad. Carol went to a girl's prep school in the east, and had come home on break. Her mother suggested that she throw a party, and that the mother would invite people for her. Now that's the kiss of death. Having your mother invite your guests. So Carol called me up and invited me to her party.

This was a very wealthy family. It was 1965 and we all came in suits and ties. The girls were in party dresses. So I called up Jerry. I said, "Jerry, look! I'm going to this party. It may be terrible. It may be O.K. I have no idea. Let's go, you and I always have fun together. We've gotten in and out of trouble before. Let's go!" So we went to this place. It was just gorgeous. When we got there the girls were all dressed up. They hired a band. Everybody was just standing around. Carol was very pretty, but nobody seemed to know anybody else. It was all so formal. So the band played a tune. Nobody did anything. Everybody was too shy to get up and dance.

Jerry and I were sitting by the fireplace. I looked over at Jerry and he looked at me. I said, "What do you say we kick this party into high gear." He said, "O.K. fine!" So the next time the band started playing, we went over and pulled two girls who we never met to the dance floor. Then we motioned to some other guys to get some girls on the dance floor. Then we went to the band and started requesting songs. We were dancing with two or three girls at a time. Jerry is a great dancer, and now other guys are coming down. Their coats are coming off and the girls are kicking off their shoes. We fired that party into high gear. It turned out to be so much fun, just a great, great evening. By the time the band was getting ready to leave, we were all sitting around telling stories. Nobody was leaving. The thing went on till 2:00 in the morning.

Well, Carol called me the next morning. She said that Jerry and I were the life of the party. She asked me if she got ten of the people back to the party, would we come back again. Jerry and I said, "Sure!" So Carol and I dated for three years. She introduced Jerry to lots of her friends. We became mainstays at her house. We became a whole group.

Another party that we both recall very well was at a cattle ranch in Wyoming. We had a friend named Tom Carney who dated my sister Susie, and he persuaded his father to let him throw a party at the ranch. It was a four-day-long house party. Susie went with Tom Carney, Susie's best friend went with his brother, and I went with Jeanne Roach. There were about twelve of us. "I can't believe my parents let me do this," Susie often says. "But they would always say that Jerry was going to be there to watch me. And he did. He always looked out for me."

So whether it was Carol Lohman's house or a ranch party in Wyoming, or a regular Richard and Jerry party anywhere, we just brought an energy to things that had nothing to do with getting high or joyriding. The parents were amazed that their kids could have that much fun and keep it clean.

Of course, high school was more than one big party. We took our studies seriously and sports were very important too. I grew up with sports, and with my dad being a coach, our family had gone to his games from my earliest years. My greatest desire was to play football for Notre Dame High, where my dad had started his teaching and coaching career.

At Notre Dame, we had three levels of football—the frosh for freshmen, the junior varsity for sophomores, and the varsity for juniors and seniors. I played on the frosh and the junior varsity squads as a 135-pound linebacker and center. I wasn't particularly big and I didn't have much weight, but I had the speed and quickness to make a pretty decent linebacker. We played schools like Loyola and Crespi in the Catholic League, as well as a few public league teams during the preseason. In 1964, Notre Dame won the Junior Varsity Catholic City Championship. I still have my letter sweater with the championship emblem sewn onto it. Playing on that championship team at Notre Dame remains one of the biggest thrills of my life.

All three squads worked out together before the season

opened. In 1965, I was in line for a varsity position. Unfortunately, I came head to head with an immovable object and an irresistible force in the form of one person. There was a burly freshman trying out for the team, and I lined up across from him during scrimmage. The coach told me to give him everything I had, despite the disparity in size between us. I tried to stop him on the line and the guy literally ran over me. Then I tried to charge him on defense, and he wouldn't budge an inch. The coaches were watching and liked what they saw. He moved right up and took my position on the varsity team. His name was John Vella and he went on to play professional football in the NFL with the Oakland Raiders.

Not playing varsity ball, although a disappointment, gave me more time to spend on music. When I was still doing *Leave It to Beaver*, I played the drums, and I recorded two vocal singles of my own for Atlantic records: "Wind Up Toy" and "Don't You Cry."

When I organized Beaver and the Trappers in high school, I started playing the guitar—Rich Correll was a far better drummer than I was. I played rhythm guitar, and we had a lead guitar and bass guitar as well. I learned to play guitar by picking up a book on folk music that offered instructional techniques. I practiced the different chords, pressing my fingers against the frets to help me play them well. Later, lots of people helped me to improve. One thing I didn't do was play and sing. If I sang a number, the other fellows did the playing. I found playing and singing at the same time to be just too tough.

Beaver and the Trappers included Rich Correll on drums, and Ron Kackabee, Jim Seward (Suede), and me on guitars. I did the main vocal. We recorded "Misery" and "Happiness Is" for White Cliff Record Company. Our recording of "Happiness Is" became the number one song in Hawaii and Alaska for three weeks. Richard and I wrote "Happiness Is" and every now and then, when I am invited to make a personal appearance at a radio station, they will pull out a copy. It's embarrassing but I just say, "It's only Rock 'n' Roll."

Because *Leave It to Beaver* almost immediately went into reruns, people would ask me if I'd like to do personal appearances. The first two years my parents traveled with me; my junior and senior years I traveled on my own. When I'd go into a city, for personal appearances, this gave me an act, something that people could really enjoy. I'd hold auditions to pick up musicians for a band. Sometimes, if it was very good, I'd pick up a whole band. I'd give them a list of rock 'n' roll standards they'd need to play.

One summer I was doing a show with a band called the Ascots in a big amusement park outside of Boston. I played there four times a day and signed autographs. Well, we must have been doing a good job because Peggy Maddox, a lifetime family friend who knew the Kennedys saw us perform, and we were asked to play at a birthday party for Ted Kennedy's son. It was a star-studded party with lots of people and lots of frills. What I remember most is that the security guards allowed me to walk through the gates without as much as a check. It seems my face and my blue Irish eyes looked enough like a Kennedy's that they mistook me for one of the family members.

I also did something called Six Gun Territory at a cowboy and Indian theme park during the summers. We did re-enactments of famous gunfights. The first summer I went to North Carolina, the second summer we did a show in Florida. There were about six Indians, five cavalry guys, and a cavalry officer and dance hall girls who only served sassafrass. I was one of the Indians. The re-enactments were very realistic. An old-time train ran around the place, a frontier fort, and we had real live dancing girls. We did different things. One time we'd rob the bank. Another time we'd kidnap one of the dance hall girls. Because I was with the Indians I would attack the fort and die twelve times a day—the cavalry guys would shoot us. When the histrionics were over, I'd start signing autographs.

I was more popular in high school because of the band and my cars than because of the Beaver. I always had interesting cars. The high powered 1964 GTO that Rich Correll and I would double date in was silver and black and had 14-inch slicks in the back and motorcycle wheels in the front. I bought that car with the money I made working at Six Gun Territory that summer, and I drove it until I went into the Air Force and bought a 910 Porsche four years later.

I had my first directing experience my senior year of high

school. The student body elected me to direct the Hootenanny at Notre Dame, which included about twenty different acts. Hootenannies were extremely popular in the 1960s and usually melded folk music with rock and roll.

My high school years would not be complete without mentioning *The Dating Game*—one of the most popular television shows of the 1960s They had a daytime and nighttime version of the show. The nighttime version was far more widely syndicated and popular, but you had to go on the daytime show first to make sure you wouldn't mess up. I appeared on the daytime version as one of the three male contestants to be chosen by the girl contestant. The other two were Barry Gordon and Eddie Hodges. On the afternoon show, Barry Gordon was picked, and he and the girl spent an afternoon at the San Diego Zoo. But we all did well enough that they invited the three of us to the nighttime version. The nighttime version was the big thing, and the prizes were better. (The very first time I saw *The Dating Game*, I told my mom and dad that I was going to be on the show some day and go to England.)

What happened when I went back for the night show might have happened to a grown-up Beaver Cleaver. The three of us were on with a new girl named Geraldine Gerhart—a real nice girl. Of course, we didn't know her at the time because she was the one who was going to choose among the three of us. Jim Lang was the MC. I lucked out. After screening us all carefully with questions, Geraldine picked me as her favorite bachelor. She didn't know we were actors. As far as she knew, we were just three guys.

The big thing was that you always had to use your left hand when throwing that famous kiss at the end of the show. If you didn't use your left hand, you would smack the person next to you on the face. At the end of the show Jim Lang would say, "Let's give a big kiss!" and everybody threw a kiss. One of the biggest worries on the show was whether or not with all the excitement you would kiss with the correct hand.

Our prize was to spend New Year's Eve in London. Everything was set, but when Geraldine went to get her passport, it was revealed that she was only fifteen years old. She was a very sophisticated young lady, and when it came to the part of the application for the show asking her age, she had put eighteen. Suddenly there was a big problem. A fifteen-year-old girl couldn't run off to Europe with me. At first, no one knew exactly what to do about our pickle. At last, they found a loophole. There was some sort of FCC rule that said if you gave a person a present—the show had already aired—you couldn't take it back. So they got Jim Lang's private secretary to act as chaperone.

There was another problem too. The Brothers at Notre Dame didn't look favorably at my taking so much time off to travel throughout the year. They promptly suspended me, and consequently my grade point average suffered; not enough to keep me from graduating, but certainly enough to compromise my chances of going to the University of California at Berkeley or Harvard as I had always hoped.

Flying off to England was very exciting. But when we got there, the private secretary very definitely kept Geraldine and me apart. It was a three-day holiday over New Year's, and a big photo opportunity. We also went to Cambridge where we were driven around for two hours in a Rolls Royce—some real VIP treatment.

I then decided to spend two weeks in Ireland alone. What an interesting experience. One of the priests in our church was from Ireland, and his brother-in-law was a traveling salesman. He'd go to all these little towns and take orders. He was a married man, but his work made it a lonely life. He asked me if I'd like to join him on the road. I did so gladly.

We'd drive on tiny one-lane roads to a number of little towns. When we'd pull in, he went around to contact all his clients and I had the day free. I went to County Cork and kissed the Blarney Stone in Blarney Castle, and drove through the green of the Ring of Kerry.

As a tourist on my own I got to do so many things that were absolutely new to me. I got a much more personal view of Ireland than I ever could have on a grand tour. My family is Irish, English, and German, so I was able to see many of the places my relatives came from. My two weeks in Ireland was an education quite in a class by itself.

Soon after graduation and my trip to England and Ireland, things began to change fast around the country. By 1967, we were knee-deep in a quagmire called Vietnam. Colleges and universities around the country were rampant with anti-war protesters, with violence often spilling into the streets. I saw things differently. The country was at war, undeclared though it may have been. The Mathers had always been very patriotic, and I was prepared to do my part. Even before high school graduation I was already a member of the Air Force Reserve. There would be no Summer of Love for me. Rather, my summer of 1967 was spent in the blazing Texas heat at Lackland Air Force Base in Texas.

chapter 13

From the Air Force to Haight-Ashbury

Jerry Mathers has that unique skill to make acting look easy. The great actors all do. Look at his work before *Leave It to Beaver* and you will notice all his characters came to him without effort and were totally believable. Jerry Mathers should be listed with the twenty child actors in entertainment history.

—*Mickey Rooney*

I liked the service, and I liked the discipline, and I really wanted to be Marine. My experience at Camp Pendleton four years earlier had been such a positive one.

I tried to join the Marines, but they told me at the time that a football player—a big name football player—had just been killed in action. They said that although they would probably take me, I would most likely stay stateside. Because of the bad publicity surrounding people of prominence, they wouldn't be sending anybody like me to Vietnam. So a friend of my dad's suggested that I take the test for the Air National Guard. They weren't accepting very many people, but a high test score might get me in. I took the test and passed it, placing me at the level of a third year executive secretary.

The major obstacle was that allotments made it necessary to leave for active duty at a certain time. My allotment happened to fall about six weeks before my class graduated from high school. I was able to obtain permission from the Brothers at Notre Dame to get out of classes six weeks early. So while everyone else was finishing up classes at home, I was deep in the heart of Texas beginning my basic training.

I figured if the United States fought a war, then you supported your country. I was on the side that said "my country needs you, and you go!"

Because there was a draft, a lot of people who didn't want to be drafted into the Army enlisted in the Reserves. If you got drafted, you had no say in determining what you wanted to do in the service. In other words, you couldn't ask for a specific speciality. You had no choice in selecting your Military Operations Specialty.

We did eight weeks of basic training at Lackland. It was miserable because the Texas heat in July and August was overwhelming. We'd be running and the troops would be passing out left and right. At Lackland, they tore you down to build you up. I was told never to volunteer for anything. I was told, "Don't you raise your hand, because if you do they'll give you a lawn-mower and you'll be ordered to mow the whole damn lawn."

One of my assignments was to find out how much water was being lost through dripping plumbing. So I went over to the hospital, got a little beaker with meters on it, and went to every barracks to monitor every sink. I multiplied that and came up with a projection of how much water was leaking at Lackland Air Force Base for the whole year. Basically, it was just a guess. But it was thousands of gallons that I predicted they were losing because of leaks in the toilets and sinks.

Of course the Beaver reputation followed me wherever I traveled, and while some people at Lackland were on me a bit it wasn't a big ordeal. The funny thing is that the Marine training I did when I was fourteen years old was much tougher. Air Force training four years later was like summer camp. It was tough, make no mistake about that, but it certainly was much easier than I found at Camp Pendleton in 1963. I know now, but didn't know then, that the Marine training I had received at Camp Pendleton was geared for delinquents. They were gang kids from L.A. who had been sent by the police and social workers so the Marines could straighten them out. They thought these kids would be good candidates to join the Marines when they reached the right age, because they weren't college bound. So as a four-teen-year-old I had been at Camp Pendleton with a real tough bunch of kids, while in the Air Force I was with other guys like me or guys who were college graduates. About 50 percent of the guys in my platoon were college grads, and you can bet they were always looking for all the angles—the atmosphere was like a spin-off from Sergeant Bilko.

The first thing I was told to volunteer for was KP. I was shocked, considering the unwritten law was not to voluneer for anything. KP was supposed to be the essence of "cruel and un-usual" punishment in the service. I was told that volunteering for KP blew the cadre and the brass away because if you vol-unteered for that every day, then what else could they possibly do to you? The older guys had this thing locked. I was just a young innocent. So when the sergeants came in and asked for KP volunteers, everybody raised their hands. At the end of the training I graduated, highly qualified and with a marksmanship medal.

Our six months of training was very Gung Ho! But once it was over, there was a lot of protest in the ranks. I found that a lot of people went in and tried to sabotage the National Guard. They wanted to wear long hair and they protested when they couldn't. It became a very noncohesive unit because you had many recruits who felt very strongly opposed to the war.

The day I was supposed to graduate from basic training, a request came from Los Angeles to the Post Commander request-ing that I get a special waiver from the Department of the Air Force to be one of the presenters at the annual Emmy Awards. They made up a beautiful uniform for me—they tailored it very smartly and changed my hat. I had two ribbons affixed to my uniform: one for being a Marksman in the Air Force, the second because I was serving during Vietnam.

Angela Cartwright (from *Make Room for Daddy* and later *Lost in Space*) and I presented Gene Kelly with an Emmy for the Best Children's Television Show of the year. The last thing they did before letting me out of Lackland was to shave my head. So here I am on national television, resplendent in uniform and with my head shaved, presenting an award to Gene Kelly.

I was all decked out in my military best with Jeanne Roach as my date. We had a great time, it was a fun party. When introducing me they announced something like, "Jerry Mathers, 'The Beaver,' who just completed training for the United States Air Force." Looking back, I think that is one of the reasons the rumor that I died in Vietnam got started. So many people saw me on the Emmy Awards in full dress uniform.

After the Emmy Awards I was sent to Van Nuys right here in the Valley as an Administrative Specialist with a 702 MOS. I was basically an executive secretary for my final four months of active duty—not exactly the most exciting work in the world.

Once we returned home we were constantly drilling to prevent and suppress riots. The anti-war protests were increasing by leaps and bounds. I was taking classes at two junior colleges, hoping that eventually I could transfer to the University of California at Berkeley. Because I was attached to a local National Guard unit, changing locations at this point would have been quite difficult.

What bothered me most was being ostracized because of my short hair. Because of the Beatles and other rock groups, everybody had long hair. It seemed that the only people my age with short hair were the undercover narcs and the people who were in the military. Everybody on campus knew that if there was a riot on, we would be the ones who'd be called out to put it down. The predominant feeling on the campuses was that if you had short hair, there must be a nefarious reason for it. Plus, the guys with the long hair seemed to be having a lot more fun than we were.

And there was always the thought of possibly needing to put down riots. What was tough was that they were talking especially about Berkeley or UCLA where many of us had friends. There were massive demonstrations in front of the National Guard base. When we went to our weekend meeting there were pickets in front of the gates. I felt like a union scab going through these huge picket lines to get into the armory. Some Guardsmen and Reservists suddenly changed their minds about being in the service because they didn't approve of the war. They were promptly court-martialled or given a dishonorable discharge.

I never became a part of the so-called counterculture. My beliefs and feelings were far too traditional. The most attractive thing to me about the counterculture were the girls. They were a lot more fun. They were the artists and the most free-spirited, with far fewer constraints than the establishment girls. Most of the establishment crowd wanted to get married and start a family, which I didn't want at all at the time. Also, the possibility always loomed that I could be activated and sent into combat. The times were too uncertain.

In 1968, the stage was set for one of the wackiest things that has ever happened to me. Casualty rates were mounting in Vietnam. News service reporters looking for a story scanned the casualty lists. One of them saw a name that must have looked like Jerry Mathers and sent it in to his bureau chief.

Because there are ready-made celebrity obituary files that are available at a moment's notice, the news of my death was sent out on both wire services and was prominently listed in the papers. If this wasn't bad enough, Shelly Winters appeared on the *Tonight Show* with Johnny Carson that evening. She chose the opportunity to make a political statement near and dear to her heart. A staunch opponent to the war, she started railing about how the flower of young American manhood was being sacrificed to this nasty war business. Then she delivered her *coup de grace* when she announced that poor Jerry Mathers, that wonderful little boy who played Beaver on *Leave It to Beaver*, was killed in action in Vietnam. She then took center stage and proceeded to sing "Bring the Boys Home."

Nevertheless, my family received dozens and dozens of sympathy calls. Tony Dow even sent flowers to my parents. The following day, the wire services retracted the report, but the retraction was buried somewhere on page seventeen. A few months later I was walking down the street and I encountered somebody I had known. He said something like, "Hey Jerry, how you doing? I heard you were killed in Vietnam. That's not true, is it?"

When I was in the National Guard my agent would ask me to go out on interviews. In the middle of the Vietnam War, with flower children walking the streets and even Robert Redford

sporting a shoulder-length shag, the symbol of everything sup-
posedly wrong with America shows up to read for a part. Peter
Fonda was cool. The Jefferson Airplane were cool.

The entertainment industry has always leaned on the liberal
side anyway and was on the forefront of anti-war sentiments. I
looked like a present day skinhead. The common question was
"Can you grow your hair out?" No. The interview would be
over before it began.

There were interviews which turned into personal appearances. Producers would ask that I join them at their home or
office to read for a part. When I got there they would say something like, "We know you're not right for this part, but we loved
your show and wanted to meet you. Would you mind signing
a few things and meeting my office staff or family?"

I was asked to read for a part in *The Last Picture Show*. I
heard that Cybil Shepherd, a top teen model, was already cast
in it. I had a terrible crush on her. If she wanted to call me Beaver
Cleaver and ask for a thousand autographs I wouldn't care! She
was, and still is, a babe!

I met Peter Bogdanovich and we went into a room with three
or four people. I told them that I was in love with Cybil Shepherd and jokingly told them I would play a farm animal for no
pay if I could just hang around her. Wrong move! I was only to
discover later that Peter Bogdanovich had the exact same thing
in mind . . . and was successful both with the film and acquiring
Cybil Shepherd, the girl who was meant for me.

I interviewed once with Stanley Kubrick. What was interesting was that when I walked in he was sitting *on* his desk, this
huge executive desk. I sat in a chair in front of him. He was
towering over me and asked me to read a part. We talked a bit,
and that was it.

Except for my very first appearance on television with Ed
Wynn in the early 1950s, I had never been in a western even
though I loved them. At the time I was asked to read for a lot
of westerns, but when they looked at me my hair got in the way.
Often I was told that I was very good, but that it would be too
much trouble to put a wig on me. So they'd look for someone
else with longer hair.

Naturally, when I didn't get parts it bothered me. But fortunately, it wasn't a matter of survival for me—I didn't need to work as an actor to make a living. I was busy doing other things. I was going to school and I was in the National Guard for much of the time. Nor was I a dedicated actor then.

If I wasn't going to be a regularly working actor, I had other avenues to follow. I recall what Ben Johnson, the Oscar-winning cowboy star and actor, once said: "You can survive this business pretty well, if you always have something else to do." It's still good advice.

My main goal became getting a college degree, and to use it to make a good living for myself in a field unrelated to show business.

I finally got to go, at least part-time, to the University of California at Berkeley in 1971. The deal I made with the National Guard was that if I was activated I would have to be back to the base within twenty-four hours. But when I was stuck on campus for five days because of a big earthquake, they changed their minds. I was told that I had to be within fifty miles of the base at all times. By taking advantage of every opportunity to put in additional hours, I was able to fulfill my National Guard obligation in five and a half years. Immediately upon my discharge, I applied to Berkeley as a full-time student. To my delight I was accepted.

chapter 14

From Berkeley to Banking

Jerry was like any college kid except that he drove a 1958 Porsche Speedster, never needed money, wore expensive clothes, and the professors would ask for his autograph. Of course, every girl on campus wanted to "get" him . . . and his bank account. He didn't know who I was then, but everyone knew who he was. Jerry was nice to everyone.
—*Leigh Steinberg, former student body president, UC Berkeley*

Actors are dumb and screwed up. That is what most people thought back in the 1960s. They read a script, drink, take drugs, and have mental problems. People like Marilyn Monroe, James Dean, Montgomery Cliff, Sal Mineo, Vivian Leigh, and many more well-known borderline head cases did not help this image. This was before Brooke Shields and Jodie Foster demonstrated that actors, even women actors, had intelligence and wanted an education. They wanted to expand their brain beyond the soundstage. A majority of child actors never went to college. They kept chasing the dream of hitting it big, only to end up bitter adults screaming, "Why did you, the public, do this to me?" I never cared if I hit it big the first time, so completing college was always my goal. I was already a millionaire and heck, my dad was a school principal. Education was in my blood. I wanted to go to the University of California at Berkeley because they had a great philosophy department. Yes, an actor who wanted to study philosophy! So, I finally got away from home!

I had long ago made up my mind to go to the University of California at Berkeley. My father wanted me to go to his alma mater, University of Southern California. But I decided to try to go to Berkeley for the most basic of reasons: it was one of the finest schools in the country, especially in the philosophy area. I felt that if you are going to try something then you ought to try for the very best.

After I was accepted to Berkeley, I moved there and lived in the Chi Psi fraternity. Because I was older than most undergraduates it made sense to live in the fraternity house where the guys tended to be graduate students and a little older. In the fraternity house I became the social director. It was a very educationally oriented fraternity, and there were a lot of guys that just plain couldn't get dates. So that became my job—getting all these guys dates.

I majored in philosophy. I had already started taking philosophy courses in junior college, and I really liked them because they encouraged me to think deeply. I had always entertained the idea of becoming a lawyer, and Bolt Law School at UC Berkeley was taking most of its candidates from three departments: journalism, history, and philosophy.

Studying philosophy taught me to look at a given situation from all sides. It sounds simple enough. Because I approach problems this way, some people consider me to be negative. Yet people will come to me with a project and say, "This is it," and all they give me is the upside. But when I look at a project, I also can see the downside—the other things that just might happen and should be taken into consideration. That's not negative, it's simply being aware of all possibilities. Philosophy also taught me to search for the roots of things and find out not just whether but *why* things are true. I became a great admirer of the American pragmatists. Henry James is a particular favorite. I like the idea that if something works, use it. Maybe you can't explain it and everybody says it's wrong, but if it's going to work, then that's the way to do it.

More than a few times I've made reference to the fact that I'm dyslexic. You might wonder how I was able to digest the likes of Descartes, Liebnitz, and Spinoza, or even read scripts and deliver lines so naturally with this disorder. I'll attempt to explain. It's not that I can't read, I just can't read something word for word. When I'm reading, some of the letters or entire words will drop out. It's very random, not any particular words or letters, so it makes it especially hard to read anything out loud because other people can hear my mistakes. I can read a page, and while I might not be able to give it back to you verbatim, I can give you back the concepts. For example, with *Leave It to Beaver*, people would write the lines and I would read them back like a kid would say the words, but I wouldn't change the concept. As an adult actor, I can easily grasp the gist of the sentence or speech, but if a director or writer needs it delivered word for word it can be very difficult for me.

I was able to conceal my reading problems at an early age, and my teachers never picked up on it. In the first grade, the teachers would send a book home at night and we were supposed to read it with our parents. My mother would help me with it, and I would memorize the book. She didn't know she was helping me memorize, but that's what I was doing. The teachers at the studios wouldn't have picked up on it either because we seldom had to read out loud. When I read to myself, I can read a page over and over and usually get the gist of it. I've trained myself to cobble together the meaning and read the best I can.

I was able to get through high school and college using these techniques. I wasn't an honor student, but my grades were in the B range. The same day my high school class graduated I graduated from Lackland Air Force Base, but I did not get to hear my name called at either ceremony. I was flying back to L.A. to present an Emmy Award and looking forward to seeing Jeanne Roach again after a long absence. At Berkeley, I could digest entire books by filling in words so the sentences made sense. When I come to a word I can't spell, I have a problem. I can tell you when a word is spelled wrong, but I can't tell you the correct spelling. When I wrote papers in college, it would take me three or four times as long to write them as it would somebody else. I'd know the word I wanted to use, but I had no idea how to look it up in the dictionary. I'd have a great idea for a sentence that would help my thesis, but I couldn't put in that key word. I was very frustrated.

I was in my thirties when I found out about dyslexia. It was a revelation because in a lot of ways I'd felt that I was just plain dumb and getting away with things. That might well account for why I wanted to attend a school of Berkeley's caliber so badly. Making it through Berkeley felt like an affirmation of my abilities. Since being diagnosed with dyslexia, I've learned that people like General George Patton and many other accomplished people also were dyslexic.

Today, dyslexia is easily diagnosed. It took a lot more work for me to get my degree, but I got it in a difficult subject area. Someone told me recently that my name is in the Philosophy Perspective at Berkeley. I'm very proud of that.

If I was addressing parents today about dyslexia or other learning issues, I'd tell them that if their kids are having problems in school, not to push them too hard. Pushing is probably the worst thing that parents do to kids. There may be some things that your child can't understand and it's not a good idea to push too hard. There are some kids who are lazy, so you have to entice them to study. But once they study, if there are things they just can't learn, move on to other subjects. Everyone has their areas of strength and weakness.

I graduated from Berkeley in 1973 and received my degree in 1974. While attending Berkeley, I had wanted to get involved in radio and TV, but because the campus was so politicized it was difficult—the focus was on protest, not entertainment. So even though I was a drama minor, I didn't do any productions but I learned a lot of theater history. I had to study so hard just to get by that I was never involved in the political fracas. Berkeley was right in the thick of things then.

One day we were waiting for our teaching assistant to arrive for a philosophy class. When he didn't show up we started to get concerned. Then we heard the reason why: his girlfriend had been kidnapped and he'd been beaten up pretty badly. His girlfriend's name? Patti Hearst, and our T.A., Steven Weed, had been beaten up by her abductors—a group known as the Simbianese Liberation Army.

My life was soon to change in another direction. Every Thursday night, my fraternity brothers and I would go to a place called Kips/Up Stairs. It was a very popular hamburger joint and there was a beer hall upstairs, and Thursday night was beer drinking night for us. One Thursday I met a petite and pretty girl named Diana Platt. She was a linguistics major and exceedingly bright. She spoke twelve languages and wrote in fifteen, including French, Spanish, and Greek. She graduated with high honors as valedictorian from both her high school in Vallejo, California, and from U.C. Berkeley. Her father was Swedish and her mother was a Sephardic Jew. Her father died when she was very young and she'd been raised in the Jewish faith.

It was a typically atypical college romance. We met, fell in love, and lived together for our last year at Berkeley, and decided to get married. She was Jewish, I was Catholic. Her roots were Sephardic, mine were English, Irish, and German. Looking back, I do believe I was in love with her. I certainly wasn't lacking for girlfriends, but I'd never lived with anyone before. There were a lot of so-called romances along the way, but nothing this serious. She had a pretty bad temper and was feisty, but I kind of liked that.

Of course everybody in my family and most of my friends said it wouldn't work out because she was very opinionated. But at that age I thought I knew everything and listened to no one. They also thought we'd have problems with religious differences when we had kids. When we were living together, she'd get hurt when people sent us Christmas cards, and question why they didn't send Chanukah cards instead. It really bothered her. So there were telltale signs right away.

It was a tough nut for my parents, but they agreed to the marriage, and even allowed us to be married by a Rabbi. They hoped that later on we might decide to get married in the Catholic Church, but we never did. We had a very tough time finding a Rabbi who was willing to marry a Jew and a Gentile. But all this was anticlimactic for my parents, because their biggest shock actually came in learning that we'd been living together. They figured that I was going to Berkeley, it was very radical, and that in that atmosphere it would give us more stability if we married. I think they genuinely felt it was better to get married than to live together.

It was tough on my parents. Because of my father's war-time experience with concentration camp survivors, they were less rigid about interfaith marriage. Many of my parents' close friends were Jewish, as were mine. My parents even accepted the fact that we would be married by a Rabbi and not a Catholic priest. I even mentioned that I might consider converting to Judaism, which raised an eyebrow but not a family rejection. We still had a very tough time finding a Rabbi who was willing to marry a Jew and a Gentile, although today it is not that uncommon.

My parents were a little naive. They knew that Berkeley was a liberal school and that sexual morals were changing, but they did not want us to live together before we got married. Good boys and girls just did not do such things. Last year in talking to my mother about this book, it slipped that we already had been living together. All these years later, my mother looked away and quietly said she was "a little disappointed to know about it."

We were married in my parents' backyard. Rich Correll was my best man, and Diana's sister was the maid of honor. We moved to Encino and soon accumulated enough money to buy a house in Woodland Hills. Diana was going to UCLA, studying for her Doctorate, and teaching Spanish and French at a local school.

Meanwhile, wedding bells would soon be ringing for my sister Susie. Susie had met a fellow named Bill McSweeney while working a summer job. Bill, a real nice guy, was pursuing a career in law enforcement. He also became a surrogate big brother to Shaun and Patrick, both of whom looked up to him. The fact that my two youngest brothers eventually chose careers in law enforcement themselves may be attributed at least in part to the respect they have for my brother-in-law Bill McSweeney.

Being married changed the entire equation of my life. I needed a full-time job. I'd put myself through Berkeley by taking the money I made from *Leave It to Beaver* and investing it in corporate bonds and commercial paper. Because those kinds of securities matured every ninety days, I went to the bank to decide where to invest.

Just before I was ready to graduate, I happened to be at the bank. I'd gotten pretty friendly with the bank's president, and one day he asked me what I was going to do after I graduated. I told him that I was planning to go to law school or try my hand in mass media, and that I was getting married shortly. "Why don't you come here and work for the bank," he suggested. The bank was the Security Pacific and it was the tenth largest in the country. Later it would be bought out by Bank of America. He told me the bank had a management program that lasted nine months, and that they could teach me all about banking. He emphasized that even if I didn't want to be a banker all my life, the experience itself was still invaluable because banking deals with every type of business. He suggested that after Diana and I were married, that I should go to their main office in Los Angeles, give them his name, and say that the Berkeley bank had sent me.

I was eager to learn all the ramifications of business, which would put me in good stead if I wanted to do any kind of financing in the future. When I approached the president of Security Pacific in Los Angeles, he agreed to hire me as a manager trainee upon receiving my diploma. It was a tremendous experience. My benefactor was right, every business deals with the banks, so if you're a banker you suddenly understand all business.

You learn little tricks too. For example, when I was making a loan to a hair salon that did a lot of cash business, I discovered that the amount of money they showed on their IRS returns and the amount of money they were really making was very different. The way I found out how many clients they were really servicing was to take a look at how many towels they were using. If they used two towels per customer, and you looked at how many towels they had cleaned each month, it was very clear that they had a lot more money than they were reporting.

But even as a banker the "Beaver" identity was never far away. When someone bounced a check, for example, or a guy came in screaming or yelling because he had money in the bank and the bank made a big mistake, they'd send me to deal with the person. The feeling was that because I'd been the Beaver, no one would get mad at me. They'd just be happy to see the Beaver. But it didn't quite work out that way. I caught a lot of screaming and yelling just the same.

When *Happy Days* was very big on TV, we all decided to dress up for Halloween. So I dressed up as the Fonz. Well, one of my tellers hit the silent alarm button by mistake. All of a sudden the police arrived thinking we were being robbed. So here I was behind the counter dressed up like Fonzie with a black leather jacket, a T-shirt, and jeans. The police rushed into the bank with shotguns pointed at me. I put my hands into the air. "No, No," I protested. "I'm a bank officer! I'm supposed to be here. It's just a Halloween costume!"

People magazine came to the bank to do an article on me. I was working as a loan officer, but the bank wanted me to get behind the counter to make things look more official. So everyone decided from the picture of me in the bank that I was really a bank teller, the entry level position. For years, people would say to me, "Aren't you a teller at the bank?"

At the time, real estate was very, very big in California. Because one of the things I had to learn about in banking was real estate loans, I knew how much money real estate agents were making on every transaction. Those were the times when you could put your house in escrow for ninety days, and basically make 5 to 8 to 10 percent on your money, because houses were just going up that fast every ninety days.

My brother-in-law was also a developer in Northern California, in the Walnut Creek/Concord area. I could see that people in real estate were making much more money than bankers. Suddenly I found that instead of having an 8 to 5 job each day, I made much better money in real estate, but I was never home. I worked for a company called James R. Gary. He had about twenty or thirty women in the company, and only about four guys. The men acted as the closers. Many of the people in the company did not start as professional real estate people, but were the wives of doctors and attorneys who got into the workforce. They'd show their friends around and give them a good idea of what was available. It was an interesting job and it did well for me. But at the same time my marriage was failing.

It's hard to say exactly where a marriage goes wrong. Diana was absolutely brilliant and she'd helped me out in school. A lot of the relationship at first was built around that. She was a nice girl, but we never really had enough common interests. Then because of her doctoral work, she started spending her summers in Europe. On my end, I was making very big real estate loans, and was busy looking at houses, talking to people, and writing up deals. Because we were both so busy, I never thought it was a big deal. But I finally realized it was. We were growing apart and continued to grow apart. Finally in 1978, our brief marriage ended in divorce. We have had no contact since.

While I'd been in banking there were all sorts of offers to do different movies and stage plays, but I was working full-time and I couldn't take off and keep my job. When I started in real estate, my time became much freer. Then out of the clear blue sky everything changed. Tony Dow and I would be working together professionally once again. And not as Wally and the "Beaver."

chapter 15
So Long Stanley

Leave It to Beaver: Tony Dow and Jerry Mathers find a new channel for their talent: dinner theater . . . Beaver's . . . 31, Wally's . . . 35, and both are divorced.
—People *magazine, May 5, 1980*

P hil Gettleman has been Tony Dow's manager for thirty years now. At one point in the mid-1970s, Phil represented our whole group: Tony, Barbara, Ken, Hugh, and me. He tried diligently to put together something for all of us, either a movie, a special, or a series involving *Leave It to Beaver*. It seemed like a good idea considering that since 1957 we had not been off the air in this country. Universal owned the rights, but unfortunately nobody seemed very interested back then.

When this didn't work out, Tony Dow came to Phil with an idea—that the two of us would go on the road and do dinner theater. At the time Tony broached me with the idea, he was helping me fix my car, a classic 1958 Porshe Speedster. Earlier I mentioned that I thought Ken Osmond was the most talented actor of our group, but for sheer artistic versatility one would have to go a long way to top Tony Dow.

An accomplished painter and sculptor, Tony already had several California exhibits to his credits. He is also a superb welder, having founded his own construction company in 1974.

It was while we were working on my car that Tony suggested we work together again. I thought it would be a good idea to get out of Los Angeles and preclude the down period that people generally experience following a divorce.

It was a good move. Basically I was out of the social scene and felt that moving forward professionally was the biggest favor I could do for myself. I had a house and I just walked away from it. Diana told me that she thought I was crazy do a stage play and that I had a good job selling real estate. I reminded her that we were divorced and she had absolutely no say in the matter.

So I signed on to do a six-week engagement in Kansas City with Tony. The play was called *Boeing, Boeing* and had been a movie starring Tony Curtis and Jerry Lewis.

When Tony first approached me for live theater, I was petrified. I can admit this now. When you make a mistake on television you can go back and do it over. On stage you can't make mistakes.

Moreover, live television had been eons ago when I was but a pup. Yet once I got over the initial fright and realized that I could remember the lines, I began having lots of fun. Suddenly I was single again and enjoying it.

They billed us simply as Tony Dow and Jerry Mathers, leaving out all references to *Leave It to Beaver*. One of the marketing points was they didn't want people coming to the show and thinking they were going to see some kind of remake of *Leave It to Beaver*. The promotion simply read:

"Tony Dow and Jerry Mathers Star in *Boeing, Boeing* At the Tiffany Theater."

It was a huge success. Within ninety minutes the box office sold out the entire six-week run. When they extended the production another four weeks to a ten-week run, it sold out in forty-five minutes. We played to packed rooms, and on opening night we appeared on the front page of the *Kansas City Star*.

We had a one-week rehearsal, standard for most dinner theaters. *Boeing, Boeing* was a fast moving farce about airline stewardesses. You had people coming in one door, and out the other. It was constant movement with a quick pace. If you were not right on top of it, the whole thing could fall apart.

It was a wonderful time for us. They would pick us up and take us to the theater. The theater put us up in the Ambassador Hotel penthouse. Our meals were either at the theater or a trade-out, which simply means that we ate at the best restaurants because the theater wanted to use our visibility for public relation purposes.

We worked an hour and a half each night. It wasn't great pay, but was more than enough considering that our expenses were minimal. They payed for everything and gave us a car as well.

Soon there were other offers. When we finished our ten weeks in Kansas City, I headed alone to Salt Lake City to do a Jack Sharkey play called *Who's on First*.

It was about a wife who is giving her husband a surprise birthday party. All his friends are coming, and she hires a magician to entertain for them. While she is talking to the magician, the husband walks in. Because the party was to be a secret, the husband thinks his wife is having an affair and shoots the wife and the magician.

You then see the same scene done over and over again with a different dialect and with different costumes. It was like four separate plays with the same story line and theme. You have one set with Japanese people, one set with English people, and so on. At the end we find out that it's all been a part of the magician's trick. It's a real screwy play.

The Salt Lake City venture went over well. Because of this, Tony and I teamed up again for another engagement of *Boeing, Boeing*, this time in Florida. Once again we played to sell-out audiences.

There was a fellow in Kansas City, a rock star promoter, who thought we should not do dinner theater. He suggested instead that we perform in two thousand-seat auditoriums and go all over the Midwest with a fresh play.

So we started to look for properties. We had hoped to do something by Neil Simon, but the royalties would have cost us a fortune. So we put an ad in the *Daily Variety* for a play. A couple of writers named Bob Shiller and Bob Weiscoff submitted a script entitled *So Long Stanley*.

Shiller and Weiscoff were Norman Lear's head writers, but when they had been struggling young writers in New York they had written *So Long Stanley* for Dean Martin and Jerry Lewis. At the time they had sold the option to Martin and Lewis for 50 percent each. But when Martin and Lewis broke up, the parting was not amicable and neither one would let the other open it on Broadway.

So it was an original play written by these two unknowns, who ten years later had become well-known writers in Los Angeles. By this time the play had passed back to them and was sitting in their portfolio of unused collections.

But we ran into the inevitable snags. Tony stayed in Kansas City for eight weeks putting all the pieces together. We had set designs and tons of people coming in from everywhere.

About two weeks before everything was to kick off, the promoter backed out. So basically we were left with the script which we took an option on. Since we had put so much work into it, we decided to continue and try to put something together. We had a professional association with producer Richard Carruthers who ran two successful dinner theaters in Kansas City.

We showed Dick Carruthers the script and told him we would like to do it in his theater. We thought if we did it here in Kansas City and it was successful, we could package it and send it out to other dinner theaters across the country. He liked it and came aboard. So with Phil Gettleman representing our interests, Dick Carruthers spearheaded it and put the package together.

It worked out well for us, and getting the shaft from the original producer was a blessing in disguise. *So Long Stanley* was really a piece of fluff, and could only have worked out this well in a dinner theater setting. Dick Carruthers opened the doors to his theater. It also happened to be a fortuitous time to do this play. In town at the same time was a dinner theater convention, and dinner theater was at its peak back then.

Bingo! The play was on the board for eighteen months. We

played in dinner theaters across the country: Kansas City, Cincinnati, Texas, New York. It closed eighteen months later at a little dinner theater in San Clemente, California. Because the show made money every place we took it, we were always able to take it to the next phase.

In the play, I was supposed to be a very neurotic Jerry Lewis–like character, with glasses and long hair. I decided my life is over because I'm in love with a married woman. I live in an apartment and I'm seeing a psychiatrist who lives one apartment below me. Tony Dow is my roommate and he just eloped.

The show starts when I decide I'm in love with my best friend's wife and I'm going to hang myself. The rope breaks. I try to shoot myself but the gun won't fire. So I hire a hit man to come and kill me. Unbeknownst to me, Tony comes back and brings his new wife to spend their honeymoon in his apartment. Of course, he wants me to leave. Hence, *So Long Stanley*. Naturally I don't want to tell him I'm so depressed that I hired a hit man. After all, it would wreck his honeymoon. So I try to call the hit man off. It's a farce and the play builds up as the hit man comes in and out and we're hitting each other over the head.

Now the person whose wife I'm in love with turns out to be the wife of the psychiatrist. He really wants to divorce her, but thinks that she can't live without him. But she really wants to divorce him so she can marry me, but he doesn't know that. The hit man it turns out really doesn't want to be a hit man after all, and the bachelor (Tony) and his new bride are just plain happy to be married. So everything works out in the end.

It was a crazy play, very physical and very demanding. It was fairly hard work, and we had tough times too. Once Tony, the girl in the play, and I all had the flu. We literally had buckets in the wings and we were vomiting between scenes. Then we'd come back out and say our lines. That's how sick we were. But we were troupers and made it through the ordeal.

Tony and I rehearsed for a week before we opened in Kansas City. We'd do a show six nights a week—Tuesday through Sunday. And we did matinee performances on Saturday and Sunday. On Monday, we'd move to the next city and open on Tuesday.

After each show, we'd come to the lobby, and in most cities where we performed *Leave It to Beaver* was still running on TV. Of course, that helped because we had audiences who had grown up on it. The audience participation was very interesting. We'd be signing autographs in the lobby, and the fans would have memorabilia that we'd never seen before. Phil Gettleman had struck a deal with the producer Rich Carruthers to come to each city a week before the production, and stay the first week of production. Phil would set up all of the press and publicity, which he did so well.

I liked being an actor again. It was good training, and I learned that I could still do it. I could make people laugh. It was very easy for me. Tony's big joke was that I was always doing "gorilla theater." Tony is a very precise person, and he wanted to do it the same way every night. But it gets stiff when it's done the same way. So every night, to make him think about things, I'd change minute parts of the play. It would drive him crazy, but it also kept him on his toes. And it made the show a lot more energetic.

During one performance, the phone was supposed to ring at a certain time in the show, but for some reason it shorted out. Then in the middle of a scene, a scene when the phone wasn't supposed to ring, it started ringing. Of course, Tony and I know that this is a dead phone, and it's really just a bell that people in the show associate with the phone ringing. Tony and I were both thinking, "Why is this phone ringing?" We did that staring game—I'm looking at him and he's looking at me to see who's going pick it up. I figured that I'd better go over and answer it. I said, "Hello," and Tony's thinking this is good. Jerry's answered the phone, so now he's going to have to improvise his way out of it. I turned to him and said, "Oh, it's for you," and I handed him the phone. I was always doing these little things just to keep it a lot more interesting, a lot more fresh.

After the performances, we'd party at night because we didn't do a show until 7:00 the next evening. I was divorced at the time and going out with people after the show. I'd usually come back at about 10:00 or 11:00. But the guys in the apartment complex would lure the girls from the bars home with them.

Then it was "Beaver" time all over again. They'd say, "Hey, 'The Beaver' lives in my apartment complex! Let's go meet 'The Beaver'!" So at 3:00 in the morning I'd have five drunks pounding on my door to say, "Hi!" It wasn't a very pleasant thing.

In Austin, Texas, I picked up a pal—an attack-trained Doberman pinscher. I had a brand new black and tan, 300 Turbo Diesel Mercedes. I thought I was pretty hot stuff. I took the Doberman everywhere. When you have a Doberman, nobody messes with you.

The dog was more intelligent than most people I knew. It was computer-bred. The best features of several families of Dobermans were fed into a computer, and then the best two dogs were mated. Sort of a master race of Dobermans. This dog could tell if someone lied. I have been told that humans emit a subtle scent when they lie. When people would lie to me the dog would put his ears back. Many decisions in my life were being directed by my dogs' ears.

I was on a roll. I was popular. I was single. I had a new car. And I had my psychic Doberman. Life was good!

But when we got to Cincinnati I was told by the apartment manager that I had to get rid of my dog. No way! I told him the dog was staying or we were both leaving Cincinnati together.

Obviously I made my point because the theater sent its public relations girl to see me. They told her to try to talk me out of the dog. This girl may have had a mind for business but her body was designed for sin. The manager of the theater and of the apartment building was hoping that my stubbornness could be broken down by my libido. The girl came to the apartment only to ask me out for a drink later than night.

Her name was Rhonda Gehring, and she was twenty-six years old. I had no clue that she would soon be wife number two and the mother of my children. After drinks that night and several hours of "discussion," the dog got permission to stay in the apartment—and so did Rhonda.

Because she was working as the theater's public relations person, she was in charge of running me around. Every day she would get me up at six in the morning and take me to these little radio stations thirty miles out of Cincinnati.

When we moved the show to Indianapolis, Rhonda came to visit. Then it was off to New York. I invited Rhonda to go on the road with me and she agreed.

We went to New York and started living together, which was not a big hit with my family. They felt that an "aggressive" woman was taking advantage of their son, but Rhonda and I continued to live together for eighteen months.

Cupid visited Tony Dow as well. While we were doing the show he met a woman named Lauren. Eventually they too would be married.

New York was very exciting, and it was especially nice for me. Rhonda and I were together and we were in love. It was still the honeymoon stage of our relationship, and we were enjoying the high life. We were living in a beautiful hotel, and had money to spend because I was working every week. Because we were doing dinner theater in Westchester, during the day we'd hit New York City and look around. It was all very romantic. When you do a play for eighteen months with only Mondays off, you've literally given hundreds of performances. It got to the point that we didn't need any long rehearsal time, we'd just go out and do it.

The play did very well and the reviews were basically good. The most difficult thing was doing a play that was written for Broadway in a dinner theater. We had to tone it down, and we were constantly rewriting. We found that a joke that did great in Columbus, Ohio, might not get any laughs in Indianapolis. Another joke that didn't get any laughs in Columbus would get a big belly laugh in Cincinnati. Another problem was that Shiller and Weiscoff allowed Richard Carruthers to rewrite anything he thought needed changing. Because he was from Kansas City, he would fly in some nights, change parts of the play, and then leave. But the play was a success beyond our expectations. What had started as a ten-week engagement in Kansas City, resulted in more than a year and a half run in several cities. The play was doing sell-out business. I was living with Rhonda and Tony was with Lauren. It was a good time for all of us.

One of the funniest experiences occurred when *Saturday Night Live* asked us to be on the show. The dinner theater was in Westchester, about an hour and a half drive from New York City. Rodney Dangerfield was the guest host and we were to be on the news portion of the program with Bill Murray as the commentator. It was to look like they were coming to our theater and our dressing room. But actually we had to drive in from our dinner theater in Westchester. On Saturday night a huge fog had rolled in. We were supposed to go to NBC and get our makeup and everything. The driver was going bonkers because he couldn't see what was in front of him. It was really harrowing. The guy was driving so fast we thought we were going to die.

Despite the harrowing encounter, we managed to get to the studio in one piece. We were told we would have a half hour for one more dress rehearsal and makeup, but when the car pulled in front of NBC, the guard grabbed us and raced us up the stairs. They threw us on the couch that was our simulated dressing room and the vignette began. We hadn't a moment left to spare.

I had some qualms about the skit because it was a parody about me dying in Vietnam. Bill Murray says to me, "I hear you're doing a stage play." I say, "Yes." "Why did you say you were killed in Vietnam?" he asks. I answer, "Well, my career wasn't doing well. We were doing this play, and we needed a lot of publicity. And I thought if I said I was killed in Vietnam it would bring back my career." We ended the skit with Tony and me throwing pillows at each other.

Of course this was all just a parody and written into the skit. But it's funny, even though it was supposed to be a parody, a lot of people actually believed that was how the rumor started.

The *SNL*-ers were a fun group, and they were more than eager to accommodate us. Tony and I were asked what we needed in our dressing room to make things more comfortable. "Oh, some water will be fine," Tony said. They said, "No. What do you *need* in your dressing rooms—drugs, liquor, women? What do you need?" It really blew me away. These people were very much out there having fun, and they thought we were like a rock 'n' roll band. In a lot of ways we were innocents compared to them. As a courtesy they took us out to a little cafe after the show. We went to a bar and partied there with the whole *Sat-*

urday Night Live gang. Everyone was very complimentary about
Leave It to Beaver.

We completed our tour of the play at a little dinner theater
in San Clemente. Rhonda returned with me, and we rented a
little house in San Clemente. A short time later we were married.
The show had been an enormous success.

chapter 16
Return to Mayfield

I remember this very clearly. In February of my junior year in high school, I said to myself, I wonder what those guys are doing. I meant Wally and the Beaver. The thought really stayed with me.

—*Brian Levant*

Thomas Wolfe warned that you can't go home again. But just maybe he forgot the old adage that home is where the heart is. And for most of us associated with *Leave It to Beaver*, the Cleaver household was never really very far away.

By the time we reunited for the CBS Movie of the Week, *Still the Beaver*, twenty years had passed since our original sojourn. Joe Connelly had retired and Bob Mosher was already gone. Hugh left us just a few months earlier and was sorely missed by all. Since 1964, Hugh had appeared in a few series like *Wagon Train* and *Petticoat Junction*, but he spent most of his time working with community theater and church groups.

Once in a while he would ask Tony or me to be in a church play he was directing.

The last days of Hugh's life were physically challenging. He suffered from a variety of diseases, including Tourette's Syndrome. One of the disease's symptoms is uncontrolled speech, sometimes offensive speech. One time not too long before he died, I saw Hugh shopping in a grocery store. Hugh looked very frail. He walked up to me and we hugged. Then out of nowhere he began to swear like a sailor. Every filthy word I had ever heard all coming from one of the kindest and most gentle people I had ever known. A minister no less. After a minute he stopped and said he was sorry. It had been very embarrassing because other people, recognizing the two of us, had heard his uncontrollable tirade. I have always been sorry that those people probably walked away with the worst possible memory of Hugh Beaumont.

Performing in dinner theater had been a shot in the arm for me. Appearances at shopping malls, car shows, and college campuses increased in number. I always thought it fun that so many different people could ask me the same question nearly two decades after the show's original run. Beaver fever was alive and well. Perhaps my finest hour was a Beaver Marathon in San Francisco. The rains came down and it poured for hours, and there was talk of cancellation. But when the doors opened, it seemed like people would never stop coming in. I signed autographs and pictures for hours. The late Herb Caen, the Bay Area's favorite writer, featured the event in his column.

I went to work as a disc jockey at KEZY-AM radio in Anaheim, California. I loved seeing "The Beav Is Back And We Got Him: Jerry Mathers Still Popular After All These Years" emblazoned across the Weekend section of the Orange County *Daily Pilot* on November 13, 1981. KEZY had first decided to go with Timothy Leary, the high priest of LSD, as their new DJ. But Anaheim was Orange County, the bastion of conservative California, and the station's sponsors and audience raised a furor. To attract audiences in their thirties, program director David Forman thought that at age 33 I would make a worthy addition to the KEZY staff. My weekend show was called "Jerry Mathers Gathers Rock 'n' Roll for the Mind, Body and Soul."

Between rock 'n' roll tunes, I fielded on-air radio calls from listener fans who wanted a slice of television history. My show was on from six to ten every morning. Most of the callers wanted to know what had happened to the Beav and all the other *Leave It to Beaver* stars. What I found out was just how many legions of Beaver fans were really out there. "Jerry's one of the few people I know who considers his image of the past as just being a nickname," Dave Forman told the *Daily Pilot*. "I thought it was a real healthy way of looking at it. He's a very natural talk show host."

But the big resurgence of "Beaver Fever" came with the 1983 CBS Movie of the Week, *Still The Beaver*. And nobody was more responsible for the show than Brian Levant. Brian had been a Beaver trivia buff since his early boyhood days in Highland Park, Illinois, and actually recalls watching the first episode.

I first met Brian when we were doing *So Long Stanley* in San Clemente. Rich Correll, who now was the associate producer of *Happy Days*, took Brian Levant and fellow writer Nick Abdo to the show to introduce us. At the time, Brian was the head writer for *Happy Days*. Both Brian and Nick were huge *Leave It to Beaver* fans. They had read the reviews for *So Long Stanley* and saw that we played to standing room audiences for eighteen months across the country. They decided they'd submit a script for the remake of *Leave It to Beaver* as a Movie of the Week. It was a gamble because similar past efforts had come to naught.

Norman Tokar had originally pitched the idea to ABC. We had talked about it a number of times, and ABC was very excited about doing it. But Universal didn't want to do it. On one occasion, they passed because they were going to do a cartoon feature, an animated series. But they never did.

I recall that when Nick Abdo and Brian approached Tony Dow and me with the idea in San Clemente, our thought was that if they could get it done, then do it. Universal had fallen out of touch with the popularity of the show. They collected a lot of money from the licenses, but they had stopped actively developing it.

When Brian and Nick approached Universal, I imagine the feeling was that since these guys came from *Happy Days* the thing might work. As Tony Dow says, in today's TV world ideas are a dime a dozen. Two things are important: One is a star. If you can come in with a package and you have a star they can't get, you've got a chance. But mainly the show has to have a writer who knows how to run a writing staff and knows how to produce a show. So you can have the greatest idea in the world, but if you don't have a show runner, maybe "coordinator" is a better term, you really don't have a chance.

The problem was that Brian and Nick were still working on *Happy Days*, and they couldn't do the script. So for about a year, Universal started putting out the idea for scripts from different writers. They were just getting the craziest things, and it soon became clear that a lot of these writers were just getting old scripts from other shows and throwing in Beaver and Wally. For example, one of the scripts had Beaver coming back from Vietnam in the early '70s. He comes to Mayfield and Wally is the chief of police. There is a bank robbery and Cleaver family members are being held in the bank. Beaver marches in as kind of a Rambo character and frees his family from the bank. That's a movie I'm glad the world never had to sit through.

Finally in late 1981 or early 1982, Brian Levant and Nick Abdo left *Happy Days* and submitted a script to Universal called *Still The Beaver*. Brian was so immersed in the original *Leave It to Beaver* that he knew wonderful little ins and outs to put into his script.

Brian Levant remembers meeting us:

> We had a lot of fun. We met Jerry and Rhonda, and hung out with them until 2:00 in the morning. After so many false starts I can understand their reticence. I told Tony that we were going to bring back the show. He said, "Good Luck! Yeah! I've heard that before!" I was smart enough at that time not to say anything to Jerry. The whole thing with them was getting them to trust. They are careful and don't want to be exploited in any way. Ken Osmond won't even read for a part. Here's one of the funniest guys in the country, and he doesn't want to audition.
>
> I was really weaned on *Leave It to Beaver*. I actually remember watching the first episode "Beaver Gets 'spelled." I was eight or nine years old, and as a younger brother myself I could really relate to it. When I was in high school the country was torn apart by Vietnam. So every day after school it was a welcome respite from the real world. I could disappear for a half an hour into a

world where the worst thing that could happen to you was to have your mom buy you a girl's sweater, and you would have to wear it to school. Here was this little island of sanity and familial support.

Within a year after graduating from the University of New Mexico I was in Los Angeles writing for *The Jeffersons*. When I began making a list of things I wanted to do, I decided to try to revive [*Leave It to Beaver*]. To give you an idea, when I first wrote something down Beaver, like myself, was going to college and attempting to find his place in society. But by the time we sold the movie reunion, I was starting to raise a family and Jerry had one of his own. On *Happy Days*, I got to do all my high school and college stories. With *Still The Beaver* and *The New Leave It to Beaver*, I got to do stories about me becoming a grown-up making that transition. Unlike Beaver in the movie, I was a happily married man, while Beaver was divorced and not doing well as a parent. But he came around. Eventually, I think the character became a very strong father.

My goal in the movie was to watch and study the old series while preparing to write it. I was just astounded by the craftsmanship of the series, by the naturalness of the acting. They were beautifully molded episodes. Mosher and Connelly are the Mark Twains of the twentieth century.

So Brian Levant and Nick Abdo sold the idea to Universal, but Brian was not put in charge of the project. In fact, Universal hired two other writers to write it because they felt that Brian didn't have the experience to write a two-hour movie. These other two guys got a hold of it and wrote a horrible script. Finally, Universal wisely turned to Brian again and he wrote a terrific script.

But Brian continued to get the cold shoulder. Although CBS loved the script, and Jane Rosenthal who was in charge of the Movie of the Week division helped to get it on the air, the production was taken out of Brian's control. Brian would have liked to have used these producers he knew, but because they were young guys the studio assigned an old-time Universal producer. The new producer brought in a director from Canada named Stephen Stern.

Brian understandably was very disappointed. From the beginning, Brian and Nick had a lot of problems with Stephen Stern. Their concern was very valid. Universal had hired a director who wasn't familiar with the show and its history. As Barbara Billingsly would later say: "He's a nice man, but I don't know why they hired him." On the other hand, when he read the script he was able to bring a fresh insight to the show because he shot it as a Movie of the Week without using *Leave It to Beaver* as a crutch. He set out to do a good Movie of the Week, and he succeeded to a degree. I thought he did a great job.

Still the Beaver aired as the CBS Movie of the Week on March 18, 1983. If you dig up the Neilsen's for the original run, you'll see that in many of the overnight markets—Detroit, Chicago, New York—in the last half hour it was a 50 share. It garnered 65 million viewers, making it the highest-rated film on the network in 1983.

We all missed Hugh Beaumont, and I think that Barbara missed him most of all. The two had retained a long friendship. We realized how much we missed him the first day we sat down at the table to read the script. There was a big void without him. It wasn't possible to do a new show without at least a semblance of Hugh's presence. We wisely decided to splice selected moments from the original series into the contemporary setting of the 1980s. So Ward was still very much a part of the family. At the beginning of the movie we do a black and white scene at the cemetery with June paying a visit to Ward's grave in the rain. It was a very touching moment, and it gave us all a great deal of joy to have the movie dedicated to the memory of our TV dad.

So Beaver Cleaver returns to Mayfield in 1983. His wife, played by Joanna Gleason, has decided to run off to Europe and become a veterinarian. He's the father of two sons who were basically the same age as Wally and the Beav twenty years earlier. Because he'd been working for his father-in-law, he lost everything: his house, his car, his job.

He's broke and has no place to go but home. As he heads back to Mayfield, strains from Simon and Garfunkel's *Take the Long Way Home* are heard on the bus. He moves in with June, decides to go back and get his kids, fights for his sons, Oliver and Cory, and brings them back to Mayfield. It may be 1983, but Beaver's in a bigger mess than he's ever been in before.

Wally is an attorney, happily married to his high school sweetheart Mary Ellen Rogers, played in the movie (and later in the new series) by Janice Kent. He's impotent and they really want to have kids, so that was our subplot.

Although Beaver may have left the roost, many of his friends are still in Mayfield. Eddie Haskell is still Eddie Haskell—unctuous and weasly as ever. He owns his own construction company, which is in receivership, thanks in part to his wife turning him in to the IRS. He makes a total mess of renovating Wally's home, so Wally also has to move back in with June. His boyhood pal Richard Rickover (Rich Correll) is now a psychiatrist. Larry Mondello (Rusty Stevens) had a mystical conversion and is Avishnu from an Ashram. Fred Rutherford (Richard Deacon) is still running down his son Clarence—Lumpy—(Frank Bank) who works for him. And Miss Canfield (Diane Brewster) has taken over for Mrs. Rayburn as principal of Grant Avenue Grammar School.

While the critical reaction was mixed, the real appeal was that we were all back together again. There were all kinds of reunions, including salutes on *Good Morning America*, *The Match Game/Hollywood Squares* (where I had the center square), and *Family Feud*. Local TV stations ran Beaver-thons. I was the on-the-air host at stations across the country.

Some of the tributes were unusual to say the least. In Milwaukee, radio station WKTI-FM sponsored a concert, which I hosted, and gave fans the opportunity to spend New Year's Eve, 1984, with me. Milwaukee has always been a very strong Beaver town. At Huron High School in Michigan, the intramural softball team called itself The Almighty Cleavers in honor of our show. Second City TV did a Beaver parody where Ward stumbles around the house drunk as a skunk, Eddie comes out of the closet, and Beaver (who's unemployed) shoots Eddie through the heart. We were saluted in such films as *Fast Times at Ridgemont High* (with a clip of the soup bowl episode playing on a TV) and Blake Edwards' *The Man Who Loved Women*. Then there were the two songs performed by a pair of unlikely ensembles: "Something's Wrong With The Beaver" was recorded in 1974 by Kinky Friedman and the Lost Texas Jewboys. And "Beaver Cleaver Fever" by Angel and the Reruns, an all-girl punk rock group who were graduates of the San Francisco County Jail.

Then I got a letter making me an offer that I couldn't refuse. It was from Larry Flynt, chairman of the board at *Hustler* magazine. It read:

August 4, 1983

Dear Mr. Mathers:

You are invited to create and direct a photographic feature for publication in *Hustler* magazine, as part of a continuing series we are launching. This feature will depict your favorite sexual fantasy, although you are not expected to appear in the photos.

Hustler will furnish you with all backup equipment assistance required to create a top quality presentation. This includes models, art direction, staff photographer, set designer, and any technical or creative support needed.

Concepts can be discussed by phone, and when storyboards are prepared by our staff, we can bring them to you for approval. The shooting itself can be discussed at any time or any location at your convenience. It will take one or possibly two days at the most to complete.

To be sure that you are pleased with the results, you are also invited to participate in editing of the final photographs for publication. In return for your participation, *Hustler* will pay you ten thousand dollars plus expenses. We'd like very much for you to participate in this exciting and original project.

Please give me a call to let me know if you are interested or if you have any questions.

Best Wishes,
Larry Flynt
2029 Century Park East
Los Angeles, California 90067

It was an offer I couldn't refuse, but I did!

A more positive honor was being named Mayor of Universal City. As such, I had to attend all functions and meet all the dignitaries who came in. Whenever they had a special affair at the amusement park, I would be there.

Universal Studio was just getting ready to have their five millionth person come through the turnstile. They decided to make a big thing out of it. There was to be a huge gift, and all the media was invited. I was to meet and greet the family of this five millionth person, and give them a slew of awards. They were going to fly the lucky family to Florida as soon as the new Universal Studios opened there.

The P.R. agency positioned people to watch the line of visitors because they were looking for an ideal American family: a husband, a wife, and their children, hopefully a boy and a girl. A man and his family passed through the turnstile, and all of a sudden all these balloons went off. Everybody was looking at the guy and shaking his hand. They rushed the family up to the platform, this all-American couple and their two children—a boy and girl around ages seven and ten.

But the guy didn't seem to be going for it. He didn't want his picture taken. His wife was trying to hide, and he was looking a little funny. At first we thought he was just kind of shy. We got him in front of the press, and he said, "Thank you very much!" But it was obvious that he wanted to get down. We were all wondering why he was so embarrassed.

As M.C., I asked him his name. The guy gave his name, and I asked him what he did for a living. Then he really got weird. He said, "I work for the Government!" I asked him what he did for the Government, and he said he works for the State Department. "And what do you do for the State Department?" I asked. He answered sheepishly, "Oh, I'm the *charge de affairs* for Afghanistan."

Now this was when the Russians were at war with Afghanistan, so the guy could have been a CIA operative. He came back home for a couple of months and wanted to spend a quiet day with his family, but instead his picture ended up in papers all over the United States and the world, saying he's the *charge de affairs* for Afghanistan. That's why he was so sheepish about having his picture taken. So after this huge promotion campaign to pick our number one American family, the guy didn't want or need any publicity. Nevertheless, we gave him his prizes and the family was off to Florida. He won all sorts of merchandise for his family and toys for his kids. I personally handed him the keys to Universal City.

My professional and personal life had taken a very positive turn. I had met Rhonda, fallen in love, and was happily married. Then the greatest of all blessings. We had our son Noah, then our daughter Merci. Another daughter Gretchen was waiting in the wings in the not too distant future. Yes, the Beav was back, all right! But most important, I was now a father.

chapter 17

Thirty and Counting: The New Leave It to Beaver

When I grew up in the 1950s, I never watched television because we didn't have one in our house, so except for perhaps an episode or two along the way I never had a chance to watch the show. So when a salesman pitched me on *Leave It to Beaver*, I asked my wife at the time if it was a good show. She said, "It's a wonderful show, Ted, you ought to get it." So I did!
—*Ted Turner*

After the success of *Still The Beaver*, CBS had an option to do a series, but they didn't take it. Once that option ran out, Ned Nalle, the vice-president of Universal Pay Television, helped us make a sale to the Disney Channel for twenty-six episodes. Ned, a Princeton graduate, wrote one of thousands of letters to ABC when he was thirteen years old, protesting the cancellation of his favorite show, *Leave It to Beaver*.

We began production of *Still The Beaver* on August 23, 1984. Like any good series it took time to build. Our first season was nice, but I believe that the longer we ran, the funnier we got. In fact, Brian told me recently that one of the TV encyclopedias stated that as the new series grew older, it became more and more like the original *Leave It to Beaver*.

When we began our new series I made a conscious decision. Until then I had been doing stage plays and lots of other things as Jerry Mathers, an actor. Another turn as "Beaver Cleaver" might lock me into the character as an adult. At first, to the dismay of the other cast members and a waiting crew, I refused it. If Jerry Mathers refused the series, it would not happen. Just a little pressure was being put on me.

Then I thought about it and the $45,000-a-week salary helped me make the final decision. Being "the Beaver" was something I had more than enough time to escape. I was still in my 30s. I decided that I would stay "the Beaver" in the twentieth century, but after the year 2000 I would never again wear the Mayfield sweater. The plan still is that Beaver Cleaver will stay a part of the twentieth century, where he belongs. Jerry Mathers, the actor, will continue on into the future of entertainment.

So on went the show! It was fun and I have never regretted it.

The biggest obstacle in my returning to series television was my weight. I have always had trouble keeping my weight down when not working on film. On stage you can add a few pounds and no one really notices. Like my old friend Mr. Hitchcock, I love good food. Not junk food. Gourmet food. You give me the name of a city and I know it by its best restaurants. Plus, I didn't exercise much in those days, so I was looking a bit like a beaver, maybe storing up fat for a big winter.

Universal decided that I had to lose fifty pounds for the new series! They didn't want me to look healthy. They wanted me *thin*. They hired a personal trainer for me. I had to get up at 3:00 in the morning to get to the studio by 4:00. Jane Fonda's personal trainer worked with me. They had me doing everything. For the first month it was practically an all-liquid diet. Then it was mainly aerobics. Finally, I found a trainer who worked out at Malibu. He had me run a mile, then walk a mile. We did this for three hours a day. He put me on a liquid diet of lemonade and maple syrup for ten days. Then I was put on a diet of 750 calories a day. We continued this routine for two years. Finally, I got down to 145 pounds.

I was exercising seven days a week and sometimes didn't get home until nine at night. Rhonda would meet me at the door in some Fredericks of Hollywood outfit, and all I would fantasize about was food. Maybe if Rhonda would have dressed up as a truffle or a chocolate souffle I would have been interested. Damn. It was at moments like this that I promised myself I would never do another television series again. It was also at moments like this that I think Rhonda began to get angry at the whole celebrity thing. The public demand for how Beaver Cleaver should look "for them" had now entered our private life.

They also made me sign a waiver that I was doing this out of choice. I'd get up in the morning and have a cup of coffee. At lunch I'd have what seemed like three ounces of broiled chicken and three ounces of broccoli. At dinner I could have a baked potato with nothing on it. I got down to the desired weight all right, but once the series was over the weight immediately came back.

The most exciting thing about the new series was working with the old gang again: Barbara, Tony, Ken, Frank, Rich, and all the rest. June Cleaver had evolved into a modern matriarch who helps Beaver raise his two sons, attends college classes, holds a seat on the Mayfield City Council, and even goes out on dates. Ken Osmond returned to recapture the immortal role of Eddie Haskell. If the series did nothing else it was an excellent vehicle for Ken to show that his acting talents were as sharp as always.

"I was pretty excited about it," Ken said after making the Movie of the Week. "I was earning blue-collar wages as a cop. It wasn't astronomical wages that I got for the movie, but for a policeman's pay it was great for me. I was a little tentative not knowing if Eddie was still there. As it turned out, it was as big a surprise to me as it was to anybody, but Eddie *was* still there. I kind of fell back into the character. It felt good."

Eddie had lost nothing. In fact, for wisecracks and creepiness he established new frontiers in the *New Leave It to Beaver Show*. His TV son Freddie Haskell was a chip off the old obnoxious block, a true creep who shared Eddie's demeanor and that irritating laugh known as the "Eddie cackle." Freddie is an elegant, smooth-talking version of the classic Eddie Haskell. Freddie Haskell was played in the series by Ken's oldest son, Eric Osmond. Ken's youngest son Christian played Eddie's youngest son Bomber. He too had all the makings of an Eddie in training when Eddie and his wife Gert, played by Ellen Maxted, sent him away to military school.

Casting Janice Kent as Mary Ellen Rogers Cleaver, Wally's wife, was an excellent choice. A superb actress, Janice was born in Plainfield, New Jersey, and studied and performed in New York before coming to Los Angeles in 1980. A working actress in Los Angeles, she was on her way to London to study at the British American Drama Academy when she first auditioned and was awarded the role of Wally's wife in *Still The Beaver*. Janice is a classical actress by training, and she brought that special quality to the role of Mary Ellen.

"Since the age of five I knew I wanted to be in show business," says Janice. "I grew up watching *Leave It to Beaver* and was a big Beaver fan. Never in a thousand years did I imagine that I'd be working with the Cleavers one day, and be married to Wally who I had such a big crush on as a kid."

On the *New Leave It to Beaver*, Wally's impotence is a thing of the past, and he and Mary Ellen are happily married and the parents of two children, Kelly and Kevin.

What a big thrill to see Cheyrl Holdridge once again. Beautiful and blond as Julie Foster in the original show, Julie returns to Mayfield still blond, still beautiful, and still with eyes for Wally. At the class reunion she tries to use her seductive charms, to no avail, on the happily married Wally. A former Mouseketeer and genuinely nice person, Cheryl appeared in two episodes on the *New Leave It to Beaver*.

Another wonderful aspect of the show were the youngsters, the next generation of Cleavers. Kip Marcus, who played my eldest son Ward, was born in New York City and raised in Connecticut. In 1983, he landed a job as the understudy to the lead in the Broadway revival of *Oliver*. While he was working on Broadway, Kip saw an announcement for the search for actors to play my children in the new show. Although he was the last of several hundred young actors to audition for the part, he was the only one flown to Los Angeles to be screen tested for the role he won.

Kip is currently living and working in New York, where he was in the Broadway production of *Les Miserables*. I remember his great sense of humor. When asked once to say something about our 30th anniversary in 1987, he answered, "There's very little more important than our 30th anniversary—except the fact that I'm getting my driver's license soon."

Kaleena Kiff also bucked heavy competition en route to the show. A natural for the role of Kelly, Wally and Mary Ellen's daughter, Kaleena was selected from 800 prospective young actresses auditioning for the part.

John Snee, who played my youngest son Oliver on the new series, was part of a family affair. His father, Dennis Snee, was a talented staff writer on the show, and the co-writer of Rodney Dangerfield's *Back to School*. Born in Wichita, Kansas, John moved to Los Angeles with his family and began acting professionally in 1978. Today he lives in Berkeley, California.

The casting of Eric Osmond as Freddie Haskell was a real bonus for all of us, and well deserved. I know that Kenny and his wife Sandy never pushed Eric into acting, but like his dad the talent was there all the time. And make no mistake, although he had just a brief appearance in *Still The Beaver*, nepotism never entered the picture when it came to the new series. He met stiff competition for the role of Freddie Haskell, and he secured the part only after rigorous auditions of thousands of actors. A graduate of USC Film School in three years with extremely high grades, Eric entered the production end of the business, and today works for Brian Levant on such features as *Beethoven II* and *The Flintstones*.

The new series gave him "a chance to show the world what the Haskells are really all about," Eric insists. "As for practicing the Eddie cackle some 50,000 times, it's probably not as anal and psychotic as it makes me seem. The original series was just a terrific show. It's simple and amazingly complex at the same time."

One of the deepest personal and professional delights was meeting up with Norman Abbott again. Norman directed some episodes of the new series, and of our three main directors on the original show, Norman is the only one to have bridged both series.

Norm and I talked about everything from the real estate market to his many years in show business. Norm, a brilliant director himself, was enamored with the work of his predecessor

Norman Tokar. According to Norman Abbot, Norm Tokar was the guy who was responsible for the show's success, and established the right attitude to keep everything on kilter. While Joe Connelly and Bob Mosher did an excellent job of writing and translating the show to TV, he insists it was Norman Tokar to whom he tips his hat in deepest admiration.

We talked about David Butler, who taught me so much about comedy. As a kid, I asked David Butler how he was able to get the camel to spit at Bob Hope in *The Road to Morocco*, one of the funniest things I've ever seen in a movie. David Butler told me it was all an accident and simply happened by chance. It was a first take and Hope and Crosby were singing when just at the appropriate moment the camel turned his head and spit in Bob Hope's face.

Norman Abbott came up through the ranks of live TV and worked with the very best in the business. He recalled our assistant director Dolph Zimmer, whom he warmly referred to as "Zimmy." Dolph Zimmer was the only assistant director we ever had on the original series. He was a very interesting fellow. During World War I Dolph was driving an ambulance when he took a full burst of shrapnel through his stomach. Short, stout, and an inveterate pipe smoker, Dolph Zimmer was the bedrock of the show. He made sure we all toed the line, and that everything on the set proceeded smoothly. If anyone got out of line, Zimmy would take care of it. What I didn't know was that Dolph Zimmer came to Joe Connelly and Bob Mosher from Metro, where he did all the Clark Gable pictures. There wasn't anyone better or more efficient at his trade, and I truly feel he was the unsung hero of our show.

When the Disney Channel first started looking for a new, clean-cut show for its cable channel, they joint-ventured the series with Universal—the first time these two media giants ever worked together. We became the number one show on the Disney Channel. We did all kinds of PR for them, going to different cities to get people to subscribe to the Disney Channel. Maybe it was my imagination—or the fact that a fellow in a mouse suit can't sign autographs—but I often got more applause than Mickey at the events.

But later, Universal and Disney got into a fracas over Universal deciding to open up a theme park in Florida. It had nothing to do with the *New Leave It to Beaver Show*, but it was an old-fashioned clash of corporate egos. The marriage between Disney and Universal was beyond repair and we were caught in the corporate divorce. We went from being Disney's number one show one day to being canceled the very next day.

We did a few more shows, for which Universal put up the money. Then we were rescued by Ted Turner. He came in and made the largest order in television history for 76 episodes of the *New Leave It to Beaver Show*. We were all very grateful and very indebted.

I like Ted Turner, and my association with him predates the new series. In the late 1970s I was doing a promotion for a radio station in the Atlanta area, when Ted Turner called up the station and asked if I'd like to be his guest at a Braves game. (I might add that the station involved didn't belong to Ted Turner.) I found Ted to be an interesting individual with a lot to say. I knew he was a southern gentleman and that he had won the America's Cup, but he was very down to earth. We talked about *Leave It to Beaver* and the America's Cup, and we exchanged lots of stories. He's not your typical media mogul.

So Ted Turner came to Hollywood and we had a huge party for him in front of the outdoor *Leave It to Beaver* house on the back lot. It was a gigantic media event. I gave him a Mayfield sweater and made him an honorary citizen of Mayfield, just as I did years later for George Foreman on the *Tonight Show.*

We moved the cast and crew to Orlando, Florida, when Universal was in the process of opening its new studio for the last year of the show. Universal had drained about 600 swamp-filled acres for its theme park, but construction was way behind schedule. When we arrived, there was little except a huge slab of cement with two big state-of-the-art soundstages, and nothing around it.

The whole complex was encircled by a cyclone construction fence, and construction people were working like mad. One day a guy asked us which gate we drove into. We explained that the condominiums we were living in were down the street, and that we turned into a particular gate because it was closest. The next day there was a sign over the gate that said "Artists' Entrance." Anything we did set a precedent for this studio. Ron Howard came in with Steve Martin and Mary Steenburgen to do the film *Parenthood* on the other soundstage. Then they moved away and we were alone again. Finally, Nickelodeon moved in to do one of its live shows.

The reason they took us to Florida was to legitimize the studio by bringing in its classic production. Frank Bank, old Lumpy, doesn't like to fly, so when he was due to shoot an episode he'd drive all the way from his home in Rancho Mirage, California, to Orlando, Florida. We had moved everything down here, and Universal was two to three years behind schedule. If the show continued, it would have meant staying there another three years under these conditions. Universal considered moving the sets back to Los Angeles for a while, but the cost would have been prohibitive. I think that was one of the big reasons the show was canceled.

I was given the opportunity to direct about half a dozen episodes in the new series. I wasn't exactly a novice, and I do consider myself a good director. My first stab at directing was when we did *So Long Stanley*. In each city we had to rearrange the play for that particular dinner theater stage. Some were theaters in the round, others were thrust stages or proscenium arches. We had to set up the props and make the change from one theater to the next.

I like directing. It's always a challenge to read the writer's vision, then carry it out in your own way. The director is a very powerful person in the completion of a film. He has what's called the "director's cut," but that's not always what the audience sees because the producer owns the film and has ultimate control. But the director gets to have his cut.

In the *New Leave It to Beaver Show*, I hold the record for the fastest show ever made, the most setups in a day, and the most pages ever shot in a day. It was easy directing people I worked with because I was very familiar with their acting habits and methods. I did some crazy things too. There was one scene where Barbara is supposed to be going off to college. At the tag, which is the very end of the show, she says she's off to a college party. In a takeoff from *Animal House*, I have her walking out in a short Roman outfit yelling "Toga, Toga!" It was no big thing, but when I suggested it to the writers they said, "She'll never do that, she won't wear this short sheet." When I asked her she didn't hesitate. "Oh, sure! That sounds like fun," she said. The wardrobe lady made up something very elegant for her to wear.

Tony Dow both directed and wrote some of the episodes. It was good training for the two of us, a wonderful learning experience for Tony and me. Today, Tony is a fine director, with many nice credits under his belt.

Basically I thought the new series was good, but the problem comes when people try to compare it to the original. It's impossible to improve on a classic, and any attempt to do so would prove futile. Yet I'd be less than honest if I said that I was completely satisfied. Because I had no creative control over the show, I feel that sometimes there was too much of an effort to make it commercially successful. What I mean is that they'd put in what in the trade we call a "bumper." A bumper is a ten- to twenty-second spot that will appear on the network to urge people to watch the show. It's shown to pique people's interest. Because of this we had these little dream sequences included in the show, which would never have been in the original series. For example, June dreams that she's really Eddie Haskell, and we all had to do the Eddie Haskell cackle. It had nothing to do with the theme of the story.

The writing style was different from that of Connelly and Mosher. It was more in the venacular of the present day: dream sequences, dance numbers, and the like. They thought it would make the show more commercially successful. I felt that if they'd stuck to the original format, it would have been a better show. I make no apologies. I'm a purist, and change isn't always for the better, I feel. I fought vigorously against all these dream scenes and extraneous sequences, but I was always overruled. I figured the people in charge knew what they were doing, so I went along with the program. But they knew I didn't like those things. And I wasn't at all sure that it made the program more commercial.

In fact, there was a dance sequence in one of the episodes that I didn't want to be a part of. My daughter Gretchen was due to be born by cesarean section. So I made sure the dance sequence was filmed on the day we scheduled the cesarean section. That's why I'm not in high hat and sequined suit for the dance sequence at the malt shop. I called up that morning and said, "I'm really sorry and I know it's all set today, but I'm at the hospital and the baby is about to be born." Because they needed four people they put Janice Kent in my place.

In a lot of ways, I was the rebel of the show because I was a purist and the others felt differently. I don't know if they were right or wrong, but at the time they said that all this made the show more commercial. It didn't cause a whole lot of problems, but I feel that they didn't stick close enough to the original concept. Brian Levant felt it should be more like *Happy Days. Happy Days* has all sorts of musical numbers (which could be set in Arnold's Malt Shop, instead of being staged as complete fantasy numbers), and Brian loves that sort of thing, but I don't. It was just a difference of opinion.

No matter the merits and demerits of the new series—and the merits far exceed the demerits—nothing can mitigate the excitement of the show's 30th anniversary celebrations in 1987. The reception was extraordinary. The celebration began in early 1987, and included honors from the Governor of the State of Florida. Tony Dow and I were named Grand Marshals of the Indianapolis 500. There was a salute to *Leave It to Beaver* in the pre-game festivities at Super Bowl XXI between the Denver Broncos and New York Giants. In addition to being Honorary Mayor of Universal City, I was named Honorary Mayor of Beverly Hills as well.

Other activities included appearances at the Museum of Broadcasting in New York and the UCLA film school. When we were in New York, one of the things I most wanted was to go to the New York Stock Exchange. Well, the PR agency called up and I was able to get a private tour of the Stock Exchange. I considered this a big honor because it's so hard to get on the Exchange floor. But when I went around to the different commodity trading pits, I had to leave the floor because so many of the brokers asked for my autograph that worldwide gold trading actually stopped. A story appeared in the *Wall Street Journal* about how I disrupted world trading.

We appeared in dozens of television shows, parades, and special events. Worldwide merchandising of "Beaver" included posters, buttons, party favors, toys, T-shirts, Hallmark cards and calendars, and commercials. Tony and I became the first nonathletes to be on a box of Kelloggs Corn Flakes. The *New Leave It to Beaver* spawned its own line of merchandise as well. So great was our popularity that an estimated eighty regional and national Beaver fan clubs were in operation around the country. Not to be outdone, Universal Studios Tour planned a daylong party to celebrate the occasion.

When the series ended in 1989, we all felt a definite sadness. Once again our TV family was exiting the secure confines of Mayfield to newer avenues and arenas. I know that I'm speaking for everyone—Barbara, Tony, Ken, Frank, Janice, Richard, Kip, Kaleena, Eric, and John, as well as Brian and our assistant producer Fred Fox—when I say we all took a slice of Mayfield with us that day, and that far more will always stay with us than we ever left behind.

We did 105 episodes of the *New Leave It to Beaver* with the movie *Still The Beaver* cut into four separate shows. The magic number for any situation comedy is 100. As a rule of thumb, 300 pilots are made a year, twelve get shot, six get on the air, one survives. So there's a total of 334 Beaver episodes with both shows combined, which puts us very close to the top of the charts. Quite an accomplishment, I'd say.

chapter 18

Pastimes and Hobbies

Leave It to Beaver works, and continues to work, because they are likable characters, and they are not reaching too far for the jokes. Even as a young guy, I used to feel some competitive twinges when I was watching the show, and trying to compare my character with Jerry's. As a young guy, you want to try to be as good as possible, and compare yourself with others who are doing what you are doing.
—*Ron Howard*

During the past forty years many people have asked me about my fascination with fast cars and guns. Some people collect stamps or coins. I have always liked weapons, music and cars. In case of war, my home would be a safe haven. I don't view a gun as something that should always kill people. They were something that helped our ancestors feed their children or protect our country. Shooting is also a sport. So if you think I walk around in ill-fitting army fatigues all day and spend my summer in a remote Montana cabin, don't worry about it.

I have always been interested in the outdoors. From the time I was two years old I was living inside a studio soundstage. Musty, dusty, hot lights. Consequently, I didn't get much of a chance to go out during the week and run around. A fast car gives you freedom. Guns are for hunting in the wilderness, where you are at peace. And music frees the soul.

During the filming of *Leave It to Beaver* I was influenced by the presence of Joe Connelly and Bob Mosher. With their contrasting styles, both men were strong male role models for me. Joe Connelly collected guns and Bob Mosher collected cars, so it's no small wonder that I too became a collector of guns and cars. When I was ten years old, Mr. Connelly gave me a Winchester 30-30 to take apart. Recently, I did a benefit charity event for the Cody Gun Museum in Wyoming, the biggest gun museum in the United States. The museum let me trace where and when that gun was shipped from the Winchester Company, and I was able to trace it back to 1873.

Whenever I'd get a gun, I'd take it apart and put it back together again. Because some of these guns, like my Winchester 30-30, have certain impediments that curtail their ability to fire, you don't necessarily bring them back to shooting condition. But I love working with my hands and seeing how things work. I like to look at all the mechanisms, and see how one spring, one cog, or one lever, can make something move—all these little intricacies. From these basics I started collecting.

When people on the show asked me what I wanted for Christmas, I'd say a gun or a knife because most of the men were World War I or World War II veterans. This was the late 1950s, and World War II wasn't that far in the past. These guys all had souvenirs that they'd brought back from the two world wars army that were usually stored in garages and trunks. Norman Tokar was a USO performer during World War II, and he was able to obtain a German dress bayonet, which he gave me as a birthday present.

I remember a wonderful story that Norman told me about his World War II days. He was performing when an enemy bomber came over. Everyone dove for cover, and Norman was the only person who dove under a truck. After the bombing raid, people looked at him and said, "You're from the USO, aren't you?" Because he was in uniform, he wondered how they knew. "Because only somebody as stupid as you would hide under a gasoline truck," they said. Max Stengler, our head cameraman, had been in World War I. He gave me a felt dress helmet he had taken off a German prisoner. He also gave me a beautiful set of brass knuckles with a triangular pointed blade, which he fought somebody for, maybe even killed him, he said. All these things that people gave me would come with a story.

I also got a lot of collectibles from the studio wardrobe. Vince Dee, who was head of wardrobe, would let me into the wardrobe room where they had a huge array of World War I and World War II uniforms. Vince let me take insignias and medals off these uniforms.

A good section of my collection was stolen when I was eighteen years old. I never thought anybody would want to steal my collection, and I was very glad to show it to people. Tony Dow had given me my first shootable gun, a single shot Winchester 22, when I was twelve. I had a lot of these things on the walls of my parents home. While I was in Hawaii my parents called me to tell me that their house had been broken into, but only my guns, knives, and helmets had been stolen. Today, my collections are stored away in safes. Anybody who owns a gun must secure it in a safe place. When it's not in your immediate control, it must be stored under lock and key.

I love to hunt and I've done a lot of it. A few years ago I went to Warsaw, Missouri, for a four-day celebrity turkey shoot. Almost every gun stock (the wood at the end of a gun) in the United States is made in Warsaw. One well-known celebrity at the shoot was Ben Johnson. In addition to having been an Oscar-winning actor (*The Last Picture Show*), Ben was a real cowboy and a good shot. He was also a very nice guy. He got himself a turkey in the shoot, something that I failed to do.

One of the best celebrity events is the Charlton Heston Celebrity Shoot, which is sponsored in conjunction with the NRA. I attended the shoot for nine years until it went on hiatus in 1996. The money raised by the event was used to sponsor the Olympic Shooting team. Not everybody who participates is an NRA member—some people have never fired a gun. You can participate in different events like pistols, sporting clay, and trap. You break off into teams based on skill and experience. I won the trap shooting one year, but what interests me most is the mechanics of firearms and their history.

Many of these people are great shots. If I was pressured to name the best I would start with the "King of the Cowboys," Roy Rogers. I once saw Roy Rogers hit three hundred clay pigeons in a row without a miss. He would have hit more if his wife, Dale Evans, didn't say in her very soft way, "Roy, c'mon honey, let someone else have a turn." Thanks, Dale! Your husband would still be shooting to this day.

Robert Stack is another great shot. Bob was born with a silver spoon in his mouth and a shotgun in his hand. Bob was an Olympic shooter and has given me a lot of coaching along the way. A star of *The Untouchables* and *America's Most Wanted*, I would not want to be at the wrong end of a shoot-out with Robert Stack. Charlton Heston is also a fine shot as is Tom Selleck, but none could compare with Roy Rogers in his prime.

All right. Some of you are reading this and thinking how dangerous guns are, especially around children. Every day, especially in our major cities, young kids are killed on our streets with guns. Wake Up, America! A gun is no better or worse than the person who owns it. If a fourteen-year-old gang member has a gun, the police should lock up the kids' parents. The parents know he or she has it. They know that the kid has no training with it. They know what it MIGHT be used for. And a handgun in the city is not used for hunting anything but people.

My brothers are law enforcement officers, and I worry about them. They're on the streets all the time fighting the bad guys, and you bet I worry that some person might get an assualt rifle and harm them. But criminals are going to find these weapons anyway through illegal means. With all the places you can get such weapons, you'll never be able to keep criminals from obtaining them.

Music has been a great source of pleasure for me. Since I was a youngster, music has been a big part of my life, both personally and professionally. I played the drums as a young boy. A fellow came to the house one day to talk about producing one of my records. I ended up with another record company and the fellow never did produce any of my records, but he managed to do very well for himself as a singer, an entertainer, and a congressman. His name was Sonny Bono. I was saddened when Sonny recently died in a freak ski accident.

One of the advantages of living in Southern California, the stretch from Los Angeles south to San Diego, is the sheer volume and quality of entertainment available. In 1966, Tony Dow and

I went on a double-date to see the Turtles, one of our favorite groups, at the Whisky-a-Go-Go. But we were just blown away by the house band and its lead singer who opened the show. The group was from the UCLA film school, and Tony and I both agreed they were far more talented than the Turtles. When this group played a song called "Light My Fire," we went into orbit. That was the night that Tony and I first saw The Doors and lead singer Jim Morrison.

I'm a big fan of Frank Sinatra, and from my parents' era I like the Andrews Sisters. Fats Domino from the 1950s is another favorite. But my favorite group of all time has to be Cream with Eric Clapton, Jack Bruce, and Ginger Baker.

I have always loved cars. Universal Studios used to have a huge warehouse filled with them. They had cars from every country for every type of film or television show. Every possible make and model. If someone was making a film on the Universal back lot, which was supposed to be France in 1964, they would have a 1964 Citroen convertible waiting in the warehouse. Every car was in mint condition.

Of course, if I hung around the warehouse long enough somebody would let me sit in one of them and later maybe drive it down a back lot fire road. Mr. Lou Wasserman, the founder of MCA/Universal, would have gone nuts if he had known a twelve-year-old kid was driving a rare Duesenberg on the lot. I am sure he would have been worried about my safety as well as the invaluable car.

Jack Webb, a great actor and the creator of of *Dragnet, Emergency!, Adam 12, Project Blue Book*, and other shows once caught me lot cruising in a convertible 1959 300SL Mercedes-Benz. It had been used in the Doris Day and Rock Hudson movie *Pillow Talk*. I was in the car with a mechanic from the warehouse. We were only driving in first gear at about five miles per hour. As I turned a corner I almost ran into Mr. Webb in a new Fleetwood Cadillac. Mr. Webb was a close friend of both Mr. Lou Wasserman and Mr. Paul Donnelly, the studio's second-in-command and its vice-president and head of production for both film and television, two individuals who could make even the biggest stars at the studio shudder in fear.

In his best Detective Joe Friday voice, Mr. Webb growled, "I don't see anything now, young Mr. Mathers, if you promise me I will never see or hear of anything like this again."

I nodded my head. Mr. Webb drove off and the mechanic figured he had greased his last Universal car. I never took out another car. Mr. Webb never told his buddies in the MCA/Universal black tower and the guy in the car warehouse didn't lose his job.

I have gone through a few cars. A 1964 Pontiac GTO was my first car. The came a 912 Porsche, a Porsche Speedster, a 1967 Camaro and a Mercedes 450SL. There were a few years with boring family Mercedes-Benz models until finally returning to my present Porsche. I have always enjoyed cars that I can work on myself. Only about six guys in the world know how to work on a Maseratti. But average guys can have fun with a Porsche.

I really enjoy taking things apart and putting them back together, whether it's cars or guns. The funny thing is that originally I wasn't very good at all this, so I set out to learn how to do these things. Sometimes I have to go to friends who are gunsmiths so they can show me where a particular lever goes. But once I learn how to do a task, I can always get it right the next time. I've gone four or five days at times just trying to figure out where certain little pieces fit in correctly to make something work right.

My collection of guns and the enjoyment of cars and music gave me an interest away from the soundstage. I could talk to the guy on the street about them and not have to bring up show business. When I meet people and discuss my hobbies, for a brief moment I am not an actor. I am just a regular person who knows a lot about guns, cars, and music. Celebrities are always craving those few precious moments when they are accepted as being capable of more than reading the words they are handed by a writer. For those precious moments I am just Jerry Mathers.

chapter 19

Those Were the Days

Last week we went to the Jay Leno Show. They picked us up in the limousine. The chauffeur had a uniform and my daddy sat in the backseat with us. There was a box of candy in the backseat and they gave my sister and me suckers. I got to shake Jay Leno's hand. He was nice. It was kind of weird seeing my dad up there, but he really did good.
—*Gretchen Mathers,*
  Jerry's daughter

When I watch the original shows it's kind of weird. It's like watching home movies. It's like I'm thinking, "Oh, that's dad and dad's pretend brother."
—*Merci Mathers,*
  Jerry's daughter

I was suddenly in the 1990s. When *People* magazine listed me as one of the most well-known individuals in the history of television, I thought, "Where do I go from here?" Another television series? Producers approached Tony, Ken, and me about a number of situation comedies if we would all work together. In all honesty, we had just finished working together for thirteen years. We loved each other as brothers, but we wanted to take a vacation from each other as well. Another series together? No.

I made a decision which ultimately affected the careers of all the Mayfield boys. Mathers was hanging up acting for a while. I would not even consider another television series until the next century, the year 2000! We had all conquered twentieth-century television. We had all made more money than we ever dreamed of. Let's take a break from television and each other and become a twenty-first-century success. Tony went into television direction. Ken went home to the ranch, and I went home to my family. My family life didn't end the way I planned, but real life seldom does. I wouldn't have changed a thing.

Today, Tony Dow and Ken Osmond are showing the gray hair of wisdom. Frank Bank and I need to stay on our Jenny Craig diets. We have reached middle age. Barbara, still radiant, remains the all-American mother. The years do not seem to touch June Cleaver.

When I was preparing to begin this book, I spent a lot of time reflecting. So many of the people who molded my early years are resting with God in a better place now. Bob Mosher and our director Norman Tokar are probably writing situation comedies for an "All Angel Review."

Hugh Beaumont, a good man who as Ward Cleaver taught us how to appreciate right from wrong, is no longer with us. Neither is David Butler, that marvelous director who showed an eager young kid the art of good comedy.

Hughie MacFarland, our wardrobe man, is gone. (Many people don't know he was Fred Astaire's best man.) My good pal Bob Dawn who spent hours with me in the makeup lab letting me have fun, has passed from the scene. (Bob's father, Jack Dawn, did makeup for *The Wizard of Oz*.) Gone as well are Max Stengler, our director of photography, and Dolph Zimmer, our ramrod assistant director.

Death claimed Richard Deacon in the mid 1980s. Richard had retired and moved to Canada. All his life he had been a gourmet cook, but he always said how hard it was to cook for one person. So he went up to Canada, wrote a cookbook, and had his own TV show, *Microwave Gourmet Cooking in a Half Hour for Bachelors*. He'd show viewers how to whip up an entire gourmet meal in a half hour in the microwave. He did *Still The Beaver* with us and he had been written into the new show. Richard had always been overweight, and before our new series began production he died from a heart attack.

Others have left us too: Burt Mustin (Gus the Fireman), Doris Packer (Mrs. Rayburn), and Madge Blake (Mrs. Mondello). And a special farewell to Edgar Buchanan, the venerable character actor who played two roles, Captain Jack and Uncle Billy on *Leave It to Beaver*. A longtime character actor with a penchant for westerns, Mr. Buchanan was also a dentist. Too bad all of them couldn't have been here to have seen "Beaver" turn forty.

The cancellation of the new series was a blessing. After seven years I was worn out. My family was worn out, too. I wanted some freedom and time with my kids. Personal appearances and speaking engagements were perfect. I could pick a state. Pick a date. Pick a time. Do as many or as few as I wanted according to my family's schedule. My children's baseball or play practice was more important than another day on a soundstage. In 1989, *People* magazine named me one of television's Top 25 stars of all time. Not bad.

Once in a while a fun, quick project would be offered. I told my agent I would not work for more than a few days at a time.

One fun project was *Back to the Beach*, which we did at Paramount with Annette Funicello and Frankie Avalon. Connie Stevens and Barbara Billingsly were also in the picture. It was a remake of those beach party movies, so they hired many of the kid stars. Basically, we went down to the beach all day and waited while they were filming.

The contract that Tony and I signed said we would have no lines, although they paid us a lot of money. When we asked them where the script was, they said there wasn't one. We were going to be judges at a surfing contest and hold up cards, that was it. However, when we were filming at Zuma Beach, they decided that they wanted us to have lines. Because they were paying us way over scale, and we had already signed a contract, there was nothing we could do. Suddenly they had handed us fifteen pages of dialogue.

Tony felt we could learn all this in the short time we were allotted. Because we were to be commenting on these guys who are not in the ocean surfing, our dialogue was basically a monologue. They gave us clipboards and we were supposed to be grading the surfers, marking down scores, and holding them up. I told Tony that there was no way we could learn all these lines. But Tony was stubborn and insisted on trying. So I told him that I was going to put the script on the clipboard and read off of it. That's just what I did and they filmed it. The funniest thing was that Tony and I got great reviews in daily *Variety*. It was one of the best reviews I ever got in *Variety*. It said that we gave one of the best Siskel and Ebert imitations they'd ever seen. And here I was literally reading the whole thing off the clipboard.

In 1991, I did another appearance that was a bit more controversial. I made a cameo appearance as the Beaver on *Married with Children*. Of course, *Married with Children* is the show that really made the Fox network, and pushed the envelope in matters of sex and language on TV.

I was in their 200th episode. To celebrate, they threw one of the most beautiful dinners I've ever seen, with lavish decor and crystal chandeliers. The episode was a spoof on my life. The two Bundy kids came up to me in the supermarket and say things like, "Oh, why are you working in a supermarket?" Then the girl says, "My brother and I are having an argument. Did you spend all your money on doughnuts and girls?"

People who hated *Married with Children* were very mad at me because they said it was demeaning and wondered how I could do it. However, a lot of people said that it was really great that I could spoof myself so well. I've always made it a point to never take myself too seriously.

The best thing that happened to me in the last five years was persuading Brian McInerney to serve as my business manager and career consultant. By the time he was twenty-six years old, Brian was the general manager of a sixty-million dollar outdoor advertising company in Los Angeles. When he and the company's principal owner were foiled in a takeover bid of another company for one hundred and thirty million dollars, he abandoned corporate life. At the advanced age of twenty-nine, he went out on his own to establish a successful business management and consulting business with offices in Los Angeles and Orange County, California. Brian and I had known of each other's professional reputation because we had both attended

Notre Dame High School in Sherman Oaks, California. But it was Brian's connection as the business manager for three-time NBA champion Byron Scott, then of the Los Angeles Lakers, which put us in the same professional orbit.

Byron was a big fan of *Leave It to Beaver*. After he got home from basketball practice, he would watch the show with his son, Thomas, and daughter, LonDen.

I didn't have a business manager. I had a theatrical agent named Raphael Berko at the Media Artists agency. Raphael was always annoyed with me because I would not go out on interviews and would only work if I was home by the time the kids got out of school. Plus, I had gained a lot of weight as a serious couch potato. I kept asking Brian if he would give me business advice. He said no. When he saw that I was over my recluse period, we would talk again. We continued to be friends as did our families.

A few times we would take family vacations together. One vacation will always be remembered. The McInerneys and the Mathers rented a huge house in Big Bear Lake, California. It was in December. A snowstorm hit the mountain the night we arrived. Brian was with his wife, Kathy, and two daughters, Marissa and Bridget. We had Noah, Mercedes, and Gretchen with us. Our girls are all the same ages, which made for fun family trips. The snowstorm had covered our front door and every street was closed.

During the next eight hours our families bonded like never before on any previous vacation.

Two years later Brian introduced me to his friend Daniel Hilton, son of Baron Hilton, chairman of Hilton Hotels. Brian was helping Dan market a new microbeer company called "Waldorf Golden Ale." Brian explained that Dan was working sixteen-hour days to get his company off the ground. As a member of the Hilton family he certainly didn't need the money. Then came the speech. Life was about winning one game only to find another challenging game. I don't remember all the words but Knute Rockne would have been proud. The bottom line was that no matter how healthy my pension fund was, retiring from work at age forty-three was unhealthy for my mind and my health.

So, Brian McInerney, with the help of Dan Hilton, persuaded me to come out of self-imposed retirement. Brian finally agreed to be my business manager. The first challenge he gave me was to lose thirty pounds and revisit exercising. I suggested that I go on Phen-fen, the supposed miracle drug. Instead, Brian set up an appointment at the Jenny Craig corporate offices. A wife of one of Brian's clients was on the program and was doing well. I thought that the Jenny Craig program was for women, and besides, no regular diet I had ever tried had worked. Plus, I was really embarrassed to go into an office and say, "Hey, I can't control my eating." If a woman is overweight, social pressure dictates that she go on a diet, but guys don't do it that way. They just have heart attacks and *then* the doctor tells them to go on a diet.

Brian set up the first meeting with Linell Killus, a vice president of Jenny Craig at their corporate headquarters in La Jolla, California. I was given an introduction to the program, a set of videotapes, and told to visit the Jenny Craig Center near my house in Valencia, California.

At first, just as in the old days, all I thought about was food, but as days passed and I stayed on the Jenny Craig "reasonable" portions diet, the hunger went away and so did some weight. For the first time in my life I discovered a weight-loss program that was changing my entire attitude toward eating. I could eat without trying to make my stomach feel full all the time. The program was working. Five pounds. Then ten pounds. Twenty. Thirty. My Jenny Craig counselor was shocked. My parents were shocked. My doctor was more than pleased. After six months on the program there were discussions about becoming a spokesman for Jenny Craig.

If a symbol of the "baby boomer" generation can admit he is overweight and do something about it, so can all the other male baby boomers. Guys! We die too young because we love food too much and we think it doesn't matter.

I had not felt so good in years. I could wear suits from the *New Leave It to Beaver Show*. My waist went from 46 inches to 32 inches. Everyone was happy, especially the doctor who had worried about my high blood pressure and Type I diabetes. Plus, I was getting in the mood to go back to work. In many ways the Jenny Craig program saved my life.

My next goal was to return to the world of acting. After a successful battle with my weight, it was time to take the rest of my looks into consideration. During my teenage years I was an actor, which meant junk food on the sets and lots of makeup. The acne and the makeup became a vicious cycle; the more acne, the more makeup, which, of course, made the acne worse. And as I got older, my skin experienced the normal wear and tear of being outdoors, subject to the sun and weather.

I had heard about laser surgery and decided to look into it. I did a little research and found that Dr. Theodore Corwin in Westlake Village was highly recommended. Of course I was a bit nervous, but after talking to Dr. Corwin I felt comfortable that it was not major surgery and that I would have nice results. I've been very pleased and know I look much better in photography and in person.

Brian moved very swiftly. Within months Bob Gartlan, founder of Gartlan USA, began the design of collectible *Leave It to Beaver* plates and figurines. The Brainstorms and Mind's Eye catalogue companies began selling autographed items.

New life was put into our business "Cleavers Catering." The small Santa Clarita Valley catering company founded by Rhonda and her partner, Wendy O'Connor, began working on television sets, movie locations and catering to record company executives. This was in addition to weddings and private parties. Having "Cleavers Catering" at your event became trendy. It was now time to grow and consider franchises in other major cities. The new franchises would inherit my face on aprons, hats and trucks, plus a great book of special, healthy "Cleaver family" secret recipes, which were fun just to order.

I actually began to write a book on food and fitness, which I hope to finish in the future.

Brian insisted that Tony Dow, Ken Osmond, and Phil Gittelman have lunch and begin to talk about common projects. It was like the reuniting of the Beatles. We had not been at the same table, let alone discussing working together, for ten years. It was awkward but after twenty minutes it was fun! Could the three of us reunite for a film or television project? We were now willing to talk about it.

Here's what Brian McInerney has to say about this difficult period of my life:

> I was worried about Jerry Mathers. Rhonda Mathers and my wife, Kathy, were close friends. Rhonda would tell my wife that since the end of *The New Leave It to Beaver* in 1989, Jerry had lost his interest in the entertainment industry. Jerry and Rhonda would rarely go out in public. It would become an authograph session. "The Beaver" was not allowed to turn anyone away. The only place Jerry could find peace was in England where neither version of *Leave It to Beaver* was ever on television.
>
> I knew Jerry very well. It wasn't that he didn't care to work. The reason he retired was that he felt nothing in the present or future could surpass the legendary status of Beaver Cleaver in *Leave It to Beaver*. Even before the Universal film version of *Leave It to Beaver* was released, executives at the studio told Jerry it would fail because to the public, only he could ever be accepted as the Beaver.
>
> I recently saw a televised interview with director Steven Spielberg. He said that *Schindler's List* was by far his best film. Spielberg told the interviewer that he did not know if he could do a better directing job than what he accomplished in that movie. But even though he felt he had done his best work to date, Steven Spielberg never said he was going to retire. Perhaps his best work is still yet to come.
>
> Jerry Mathers has yet to do his best work as an actor. He stopped being challenged as an actor when he became "The Beaver" in the second television series. Financially it was great, but professionally it was a poison pill. Prior to the *New Leave It to Beaver*, Jerry was doing stage work and some film, real acting. Then, he was called back to Mayfield. Jerry was "Beaver Cleaver" for thirteen years of series television and forty years in syndicated television. What actor in entertainment history has been associated with one character for so long? He

can play "Beaver Cleaver" while sleepwalking. There is no challenge to it at all.

In the next few years, the right film or television director will use Jerry Mathers in a career breakthrough situation. As John Travolta was able to finally leave his 70's stereotype with the movie *Pulp Fiction,* so will Jerry Mathers leave "The Beaver" behind in the next few years. Maybe he'll play an evil character? Jerry is also a talented radio personality.

The most important thing is that Jerry Mathers wants to work, in whatever direction that may take him. This is a far different man, physically and emotionally, than the close friend I worried about three years ago.

Brian McInerney was now my business manager. Personal appearances increased and merchandising became more lucrative. We began to renegotiate my Universal Television royalty agreement regarding the 10 percent of the gross income clause in my original 1957 contract. I was healthy, financially secure, and living in a very nice home in Valencia. Our three children, Noah, Merci, and Gretchen, were older and doing well in school. Rhonda had a great idea for a catering company which would focus on television production companies. I loaned her the money and my eight-year-old face. "Cleavers Catering" was born. Rhonda and I went on an extended European adventure. We reenacted our wedding vows in the Catholic Church.

Then came the bombshell. My years in social and professional exile had already damaged our marriage beyond repair. Rhonda had married me at the start of the *New Leave It to Beaver* series. Living with a social and professional recluse was not in her original plan. Rhonda wanted out. People think that being married to a celebrity is fun, then they get fed up with the hassles of it. Rhonda had found someone else.

Of course, *The National Enquirer* tracked down Rhonda for a comment. Even when getting a divorce in real life I was still connected to Beaver Cleaver.

"Jerry is NOT Ward Cleaver," Rhonda told the *Enquirer.* "He is a great guy and a good husband and father—but he is no Ward Cleaver." Wow! This was so weird to me. How can I compete with a fictional character? My own wife was seeking the type of love demonstrated by my fictional father to my fictional mother, who both sprang from the imagination of Joe Connelly and Bob Mosher in 1957.

Inside Edition paid Rhonda for an interview where she complained about our property settlement. She signed on the *Leave It to Beaver* Internet page as the "real" Mrs. Mathers for anyone with questions.

Well, I guess I could have replied that Rhonda never really was my dream girl; Miss Landers would always hold that special place in my heart. Instead, I just agreed and said I did the best I could but that nobody was perfect. The Cleaver family may be cultural icons, but me, I am just a regular guy making my way through life like anyone else.

But the news still was sad to me. The last thing I had wanted for my kids was a split family. I came from a home where parents worked together as a team raising five children. Divorcing with three children counted as a 100 percent failed marriage. I had never failed 100 percent at anything. Sorry, kids. I wish I could have fixed it. Maybe Joe Connelly could have written a solution for me.

It's during times like this that good friends and a loving family really matter. And no better time was had than on June 2, 1996, when Richard Correll and I had a joint party, celebrating our 48th birthdays, which are only eighteen days apart. It was the the first Richard and Jerry Party in many years.

But it really was quite a party. My sister Susie McSweeney was pretty much in charge of organizing the party, and she did a bang-up job. It was held at Richard's house with a catered dinner. We had a real good '50s band, and Kenny and Tony were there. So were all the people from Beaver and the Trappers. It was the first time we were all together since 1967.

We performed a lot of the songs we used to do—songs by the Kinks, the Animals, the Beatles, the Rolling Stones, and the Turtles. Richard played a lot of guitar this time, and his brother Charlie, who was director of photography on shows like *The Winds of War* and has a lot of directing credits, played the drums. We played all night. Lots of old friends who'd never heard us were there, and so were old girlfriends and new girlfriends.

It was great to see my old pal Patrick Curtis at the party. Patrick has his own production company called Curtis-Lowe Productions. When he worked on *Leave It to Beaver* he was always very nice to me. He had a 1961 Corvette that he painted custom gold. His girlfriend back then was Linda Evans from *Big Valley*, and he took me with them to such places as the drag races. I was like the little brother who always tagged along.

Because Patrick was Frank Bank's age he was in many ways the leader. We used to go to Bob's Big Boy for lunch, and if there was a girl on the show she'd join us. I was about eleven or twelve and really thought it was great. Patrick had also gone to Note Dame High School, and his mother was Helen Ward, who sang with Benny Goodman. By the time I went to Notre Dame, Patrick was a legend because he was married to and managing a young actress named Raquel Welch.

Patrick and I ran into each other about ten years ago at the Charlton Heston Celebrity Shoot. He and Charlton Heston work together a lot. We renewed our friendship and it was good to get back together. Today, the ten-year age difference is nothing, but as a young kid I always looked up to him because he was so nice to me and seemed to really like having me around.

Unfortunately, Barbara Billingsly couldn't make the party because she was vacationing in Hawaii. Once, when Rhonda and I were cruising to Mexico with Barbara, she was a bit concerned because I had put on some weight again. She told Rhonda that it was probably because she wasn't giving me enough sex. Sex burns calories, she told us. "All my husbands have been skinny," she said. "If you gave him more sex, he wouldn't be fat!"

When Rhonda and I separated, I rented Charlie Chaplin's former beach house in Encinitas, California. The 1920's house is located about an hour south of Los Angeles and sits on a cliff above an incredible beach. At first I didn't even have a telephone. I would sit on the patio reading or just looking at the view. It is never easy to find out someone doesn't love you anymore and has found someone else. I needed time away from the world to deal with the sadness of it all.

As the fortieth anniversary of *Leave It to Beaver* approached, Brian asked if I would return to Los Angeles. Once again there was a great demand for the Beaver. The new *Leave It to Beaver* feature movie was to be released in the summer of 1997. However, after careful consideration, I decided not to be a part of it.

My old friend Brian Levant, the producer of the *New Leave It to Beaver* television show and several movies, including *The Flintstones*, was slated to write and direct the film. Then Brian was offered the Arnold Schwarzenegger movie *Jingle All the Way*. When Brian left the *Leave It to Beaver* project, and the studio rejected both Tony Dow and Richard Correll as directors, both Tony Dow and I decided not to participate in the new film. Brian, Tony, and Richard had a true love of the original show and an understanding of all its characters. Without such empathy, we felt that the movie would not translate to post–baby boomers. No one felt worse about the failure of the movie than Brian Levant, who only wished that he could have directed two movies at one time. There is no question in my mind that Brian Levant would have made a very successful *Leave It to Beaver* film. Both of my daughters were involved in the movie: Merci and Gretchen were extras.

On August 9, 1997, my mother and father celebrated their 50th wedding anniversary. What a wonderful occasion and what a wonderful tribute. It started out with a Mass by my first cousin Monsignor James Peterson at Our Lady of Grace, my parents' church of thirty-five years. Then all the grandchildren participated in the Mass. My daughter Merci did *The Responsorial*. She sang "Wherever You Go." There were more readings, and my daughter Gretchen did the *Intercessions*.

There were at least an hour and a half of tributes from the family, people from my father's work, and lots of people from my mother's Council of Catholic Women, of which she is a past president. Some family members told stories about how they were so upset when movies went up from a dime to twelve cents. There were stories about how my mother and father first met. The Monsignor was also the altar boy at their wedding mass. The seven grandchildren got up and thanked them for being the wonderful grandparents they were. Because Noah was in the navy and couldn't be there, I spoke for him as well as MCing. The dinner was delicious.

The whole theme of the anniversary had an Irish flavor, so we played Irish music. A friend from Ireland then gave a champagne toast in Gaelic. It was a wonderful time.

What this meant to me was a culmination of my parents being together for fifty years. It is rewarding to know that my parents were able to stay married for fifty years. It's almost amazing today to see people who have been together for fifty years and have never been separated. Like all marriages, my parents' has had highs and lows, but it endured and survived with love and caring. It gave all us kids a great and proud feeling. One person we all missed was my grandmother Marie. She lived with us all our lives, and when she died a week after the 1993 earthquake at age ninety-six we were with her until the very end.

So it's with a bittersweet look backward that I survey the first fifty years of my life, both as Beaver Cleaver and as Jerry Mathers. Even through the difficult times, love and kindness was somehow around the corner. And through the best of times, there were always people to share my joy.

If you purchased this book, you were a fan of at least one version of *Leave It to Beaver*. You were attracted to it because it was about everyday life in an innocent, mythical town. A community where you could live. No Presidential sex scandals in Mayfield. No bigotry or racism. No weapons of mass destruction.

The fact is that Mayfield and the Cleaver family do exist, in all of our hearts. Someday there may be a *Leave It to Beaver* convention, and we can all get together and dress in our retro clothes. Even though the event is crowded, we will still be polite to each other. The worst word in our vocabulary will be "creep." It will be a celebration of who Americans really are and can be again in the twenty-first century. A national social movement based on the teachings of Ward, June, Beaver, and Wally Cleaver will quickly take over the world. A world where everyone will sit down for dinner as a family after washing their face, hands, and behind their ears.

I look forward to seeing you!

Now is the time to play catch-up with some of the people who helped *Leave It to Beaver*. From the baby boomers of the 1950s to the Generation X of the 1990s, we're looking forward to forty more years. And after that, who knows! But don't count us out. The Cleavers and Mayfield USA will be around.

Life has been pretty good for most of the old gang. Remember Rusty Stevens who played my rotund pal Larry Mondello? Rusty is a successful insurance salesman on the East Coast today. Steven Talbot, who played my brazen friend Gilbert Bates, went on to become a Peabody Award–winning producer and a highly acclaimed documentary filmmaker. Stanley Fafara, who played diminitive Whitey Whitney with the high nasal voice, is an artist in Washington State. Jeri Weil, who played Judy Hensler, "the meanest girl in the whole school," is a hairdresser in Los Angeles.

Cheryl Holdridge, who played Julie Foster, is no stranger. She appeared with us recently at a *Leave It to Beaver* symposium at the Museum of Radio and Television in Beverly Hills. Best known to many as Cheryl of the "Mousketeers," Cheryl was a trained ballerina who first appeared in the movie musical *Carousel*, then went on to do lots of work in film and TV. As the coquettish Julie Foster, she was always trying to land Wally (who wasn't?). When Cheryl returned to her Los Angeles City high school after shooting a scene with Tony Dow, her girlfriends would tease her by singing "Thirteen Candles," a play on the song "Sixteen Candles," because she was three years older than Tony, a mere thirteen at the time. Today, Cheryl is involved in a variety of charity work. She is happily married and lives in Beverly Hills.

Janice Kent, who did such an outstanding job as Mary Ellen in the *New Leave It to Beaver Show*, took time off from her acting career to raise her daughter Haley. For the past few years she has had her own acting school, teaching her students the techniques of auditioning. She takes enormous pride whenever her students are cast in a production. Jancie plans to return to professional acting in the near future.

When Richard Corell was doing the original series, he went up to our director Norman Abbott and said, "Gee, Mr. Abbott, I'd really like to be a director someday." According to Norm Abbott, he politely answered, "Sure, kid," then went on his way. Today, my pal Rich Correll is one of TV's best and most well-respected directors. Good going, Rich!

Epilogue:
...And Jerry Mathers as "The Beaver"

I had the good fortune to have spent my formative years in the Golden Age of Television. This timing not only assured me a footnote in the journals of entertainment history, but gave me a unique and insightful look into this powerful dynamic medium.

As with the character Beaver Cleaver, I witnessed this media miracle at first through the eyes of a child. Unlike the character, I get to enjoy its continuing evaluation as an adult.

Television can be a powerful tool for learning and entertainment. Or if programmed by negative voices, it can be an accelerator to our doom. A society must not rein in and hobble its most talented and experimental "wild horses." They must be free to express and dispense their "wild oats," no matter which end of the horse they come out of. However, a truly free and advanced society must safeguard its "colts" until it has the vision to realize that just because the "box" says it is so, even when it's in one's home and is a trusted advisor, television may lie. There may not have been a Mayfield, a Cleaver family, or a time where all one's troubles could be worked out in the course of thirty minutes, but this may teach useful lessons.

While thirty minutes of gutter talk, bathroom humor, and nude bodies is of interest to some adults, it shouldn't become the generally accepted public standard. Our leaders must assert their power by training this wild and lustful "stallion" with one finger, and flipping it off. Leaders or parents must demonstrate their commitment by viewing shows with their charges or children, and when they find them to be inappropriate they must commit to do something about it. Enough preaching!

I have been blessed: I have wonderful parents, a great family, and three beautiful children. I had the honor of being present in the delivery room when two of my children came into the world (one by cesarean section). When one sees a new child emerge to begin life it is a moving and humbling experience. All mankind's hopes and dreams are tied to that one life. One must nurture and care for this innocent because it is truly the greatest gift from heaven. To be able to pass your genes and your traits to another human being is a blessing. I may claim that my kids are the best, but I would never dispute all other parents making this same claim.

Gallatians 6:7 tells us: Whatsoever a man soweth, that shall he reap." Well, my mom and dad "reaped" a great family. A great marriage. I "reaped" my kids and still have time for a final shot at a solid marriage.

My children, family, and friends are all on this road with me as we streak into the twenty-first century. I am excited about what is ahead and grateful to everyone for what we have accomplished. Sure, there have been mountains and valleys, but each of you have faced the same challenges for far less financial compensation and public notoriety. I'm thinking of single moms raising kids today and the moms and dads who struggle and succeed in keeping their marriages together. God bless them. They are the true heros of our time. I want *their* autographs.

A radio DJ, at the end of a very long interview, once said: "So Jerry, I hear you're a philosopher. In the next thirty seconds: What is the meaning of life? Is there life after death? Are there other beings in the Universe?" I answered: "The meaning of life is to get through it! Yes! There is life after death! Time and/or dimensional travelers who appear and vanish because of unknown wills."

It's been a great life. Given the opportunity, I would do it again (with a few changes). But no one could be that lucky. So thanks! And I mean that from the bottom of my heart. I wish that so far I could have done more for the world that has given me everything. But I'm not dead yet. So I'll keep trying, forever!

Curtain Call: Where the Cast Has Gone Since *Leave It to Beaver*

FRANK BANK As "Lumpy" Rutherford

When the original series ended, I was twenty-one years old. I was cast as Archie Andrews in *The Adventures of Archie Andrews* right after *Beaver* finished. Lucky Strikes Cigarettes bought the show, and we went to a screening for the sponsor. The sponsor was sitting there watching the show and he said, "That's 'Lumpy' Rutherford, not Archie Andrews." I heard him say that, and the next day I retired from show business.

Luckily I was at UCLA at the time, and I was a finance major. Following graduation from UCLA, I became a broker and the rest is history. I have been in the securities business for twenty-eight years. I have been general manager of the largest independent municipal and government bond firm in the United States. I wouldn't dream of doing anything without my Beaver family. That's truly how I feel. I carried on all the way in the series. Kenny, Barbara, and I are in the new movie which was shown in theaters across the country in the summer of 1997.

We were a good bunch of kids. We didn't get messed up like so many of the other TV kids. We can thank Hugh [Beaumont], Joe [Connelly], and Bob [Mosher] for that. They were very big father figures. And they kept our asses straight. When we got out of line, they leaned on us. Barbara [Billingsly] is still America's mother—to this day.

It's not been easy being the "Beaver" as an adult, I imagine. And it hasn't been easy being "Lumpy" as an adult. I guess I was more interested in getting a paycheck, buying a Cadillac, and investing the money. I guess you can say that I was the materialistic one of the group.

When we did *Still The Beaver* as the Movie of the Week for CBS, we proved Thomas Wolfe wrong. You can go home again! We did it and we proved it. I rank the guys over anyone I have ever worked with and I've worked with some of the biggest.

Still, I don't think the Movie of the Week was very good. It had a good rating but the guy didn't know anything about *Leave It to Beaver*. He was terrible. Brian Levant knew the show and should have done it. The *New Leave It to Beaver Show* was much better than people gave it credit for. We were good, and we did some great shows.

Sometimes I think the new show should have been called *Leave It to Eddie*. Eddie Haskell was so despicable on the new show it was incredible. But he has always had the best dialogue. That's the only jealousy I have. We all have it. Kenny always gets the best lines. They are the funniest. He was the most memorable character on the show.

Some of my favorite episodes include "The Soup Bowl" and "Wally's Practical Joke." That's where they tied a chain around my [Lumpy's] car. My personal favorite is an episode called "Lumpy's Scholarship." I had almost every scene and every line in that one.

The experience of *Leave It to Beaver* was the best. Today, *Seinfeld* and *Frazier* are the only sitcoms worth watching. The last great family sitcom I think was *Cosby*. There hasn't been a hell of a lot in between.

KEN OSMOND As Eddie Haskell

I started on *Beaver* when I was fourteen. I continued until I was twenty. Hugh and Barbara were what I'd call work associates. They were not surrogate parents. They were pleasant people. I enjoyed being around them, but they weren't parent figures. Hugh Beaumont was pretty much what you saw on the screen. Laid-back, easygoing, a very logical type of person.

After the original show ended, my career went in the toilet. I was very much typecast. I did a few things after the original show, but nobody in power positions could look at me and not see Eddie. For most actors that would be a death warrant. But it's not a complaint for me, because Eddie has been very good for me for many years. But as far as being a continuing child actor, it wasn't going to work for me.

During the 1960s, I bounced around all kinds of different jobs. My brother and I had a charter helicopter service for a number of years, but it was a financial disaster.

I took six months out of the show to do basic training as part of my military commitment as a reservist. I was never involved in the drug scene or the hippy movement. They were weirdo groups in my opinion. Today I am politically active. I'm not one who goes out and marches and demonstrates, but I try to stay as politically educated as I can. I am a Republican, and I'm very conservative. Not long ago I did a segment of the show *Politically Incorrect*. My kids were even a little tentative about my going on because I am very opinionated.

It was Brian Levant who approached me for the Movie of the Week. At the time I was an active L.A. policeman. I did the movie during my police vacation time. The new show was much better than the movie I feel.

The series which came after gave more time to develop characters, story lines, and such. Was I satisfied with the new show? Yes! It was a good cute show, but it was not the quality of the original. It would have been impossible. You can't match the quality of the original. The original show had some very unique qualities.

Every day at roll call with the Los Angeles Police Department, I'd get ribbing from my fellow officers. That was constant from day one. But I love coppers dearly, they are the best group of people in the world.

As time goes by, I have become even more recognized as Eddie Haskell. I was in an incident in 1980 that made the wire services. I was shot. We chased a car thief, he crashed, and we chased him on foot. He ran around the corner, and it was very bad tactics on my part. I assumed that he had kept running. In fact, he stopped and waited for me. We got toe to toe and he blew my ass out of my socks. I was shot in the upper chest, lower chest, and the abdomen. I still have the scars through the vest.

After the show, I had many other interests. I still do cameos, but only as the Eddie character. I stopped looking for the work because if it wasn't Eddie related, they wouldn't hire me. If it was Eddie related, they'd seek me out. Jerry and I do a lot of appearances together now.

Lots of people come to these appearances. We get a goodly crowd. People are generally so nice and so complimentary. I come home from these things and my ego is really inflated. It's terrific. They treat you like a king. I've done segments of talk shows here and there. I do them periodically, and I have a little cameo in the new *Leave It to Beaver* movie.

I don't think I'd change anything, thank God. I've been married to my wife Sandy for twenty-eight years. We have two boys: Eric is twenty-five and Christian is twenty-three. I have rental properties that I manage and maintain. I am the president of a water company. I keep pretty busy.

I've been blessed with so many advantages, primarily because of Eddie. I get special treatment here and there. I have been closer to a shuttle launch than anybody but perhaps the immediate family of the astronauts. I've been backstage at the Grand Ol' Opry. I visited the White House and had a private tour, and visited President Reagan when he was in office. This was a wonderful thrill, and my visit was great. Ronald Reagan is my favorite president, absolutely. And the best we've had since I have been politically aware. I will be very sorrowful when he meets his maker.

Today it is a very different world. Back in the 1950s and 1960s, movies and television were an art form. Today, it's a commercial enterprise. It's what you can put down on celluloid as fast as you can, as cheap as you can, and make the most money out of it. It's the almighty dollar!

BARBARA BILLINGSLY As June Cleaver

I'll tell you, being June Cleaver kept me working a whole lot. Hugh [Beaumont] wanted to go on and do other things while we were doing the show. It took him a while, but he grew to love it. I was right where I wanted to be. I was happy. This was exactly what I saw myself doing. I appreciated it all the time, even when we were in Florida.

I often laugh because we were sitting around Brian Levant's office and there were some complaints, and everybody had a chance to talk. They probably hated me, but I really feel this way. I was grateful every day I walked on the studio lot. I always felt that way. I was grateful. I enjoyed what I was doing. I wasn't hurrying to be someplace else. I was happy with what I had done.

Nor was I ever a surrogate mother for the boys. Today, things are different because they are not so strict with children. In those days, they had to have a mother, a father, somebody on the set with them at all times. When Marilyn Mathers wasn't on the set, for example, her sister was there.

Charles Correll was there for Richard. So was Lyle Talbot for his son Stephen [Gilbert]. I loved them both, and we got along just fine. So because I knew their parents, and a parent is there all the time, you don't assume that role. People ask me if I reprimanded them [the kids]. Of course not!

Tony grew up first. He was older and his voice changed. We all laughed because they wanted to use that. Norman Tokar was just a great director and was so good with the kids. He had a great comedy sense. He was an absolute joy as a director, and helped Tony immeasurably. He could get inside of a kid. Tony was a swimmer and diver, but eventually got to be a very good actor.

They talked about continuing the show, and the kids being in college. They kind of didn't know what to do with it. I don't think we were canceled. I think Joe and Bob had had it. Bob wasn't doing that much anymore, and Joe had all these other shows.

We'd keep in touch and meet each other from time to time.

We were in all the parades—the Christmas parades—even when Hugh was still alive. When Bob Mosher died, we were at the funeral. I've been to Tony's wedding. He's the dearest person. Tony and I got to know each other when he was an adult because we did a show together for ten weeks in Kansas City. And I have gotten to know Tony and his wife Lauren very well today. I've gotten announcements for births.

Joe [Connelly] was a big old Irishman. A two-fisted kind of guy. He was wonderful, helpful, and warm. But he learned to put a wall up, and you didn't overstep with him. I went to Joe's children's weddings.

Ken hasn't changed one iota. He looks like the part he plays, but he isn't. He's such a nice person. I'll never forget the first time they invited me to their home. They all cooked dinner together. Eddie Haskell sat there and he said grace. Nobody would believe what a nice person and what a nice family. He was on a motorcycle in the worst part of town when he was with the LAPD. It's funny, when he would do a Hollywood Parade, all these motorcycle fellows would be sitting on the corners, and here's Ken up on one of the floats.

I can't believe it is forty years and more. There's no way it's forty years. I can't believe it, but it is. Jerry and Tony didn't do the new movie. But Ken, "Lumpy," and I did. I played Aunt Martha.

Again, if I had wanted to do other things like Tony wanted to do, being locked into June Cleaver could have been a detriment. But being well known for one part has been wonderful to me because I have been able to do so many other things with it. Even *Airplane*, where I played the jive-talking passenger, I did because of June.

TONY DOW As Wally Cleaver

I stayed real busy the first couple of years after Beaver, being a guest star. I did guest appearances on *My Three Sons*, *Adam 12*, *Love American Style*, and *Mr. Novak*. I was in a series called *Never Too Young*, which was on daytime TV. Then the Army National Guard came along. It was a six-year obligation. Unfortunately, I couldn't keep my hair long. So although I managed to do a few things, I didn't get much work back then.

While I was working on a series, I went to UCLA and took a lot of night classes. I took every filmmaking course I could get my hands on. Then I got on *General Hospital*, where I had a great time. I also appeared on television in *The New Mike Hammer, Murder, She Wrote, Quincy*, and *The Love Boat*.

Today, I'm involved in directing and it's doing very well for me. I've produced a cable movie. My responsibilities are primarily visual effects. The movie was *It Came From Outer Space II*. But I didn't like the nuts and bolts of producing. A great producer is the producer who can get the great work for the least amount of money, and keep everybody happy doing it.

I've directed an episode of *Coach*. I was visual effects director for *Babylon Five*. I've been in show business now for forty years. Looking back, Jerry says that seeing the show today is like watching home movies. But for me it's different. I can't even relate to the fact that the character is me. But I'm really proud of all the shows. They are really special. I watch them, I enjoy them, and occasionally I allow myself the luxury of saying I did a pretty good job on that scene.

I think the reason we have kept such a following is that the show really has meant a lot to so many people. We were in people's living rooms for many, many years. And the product certainly lived up to its responsibility.

I really believe that if Joe Connelly and Bob Mosher had signed a bookworm kind of guy who was interested in engineering or drawing cartoons, Wally Cleaver would have been that. It so happened that I was very athletic, so Wally became a basketball player and a letterman. They wrote the character to fit what was comfortable for both of us.

I am the father of one son, Christopher, from a previous marriage. Today my wife, Lauren, and I live in the Topanga Canyon area of Los Angeles.

About the Coauthor

Herb Fagen is a lifelong fan of baseball and film. He writes for numerous baseball publications and for such Hollywood nostalgia magazines as *Classic Images*, *Films of the Golden Age*, *Movie Marketplace*, *Filmfax* and *Remember*. Born and raised in Chicago, he now lives and works in Walnut Creek, California.